22334

D0493736

R

R

This item must be returned
no later than the last date
stamped above.
**Fines are charged if items
are returned late.**

Learning Resource Centre

New Road
Havant
Hants PO9 1QL

Tel: 023 9271 4045
Email: LRC@havant.ac.uk

access to history

Second Edition

RIVALRY *and* ACCORD: INTERNATIONAL RELATIONS 1870–1914

John Lowe and
Robert Pearce

Hodder & Stoughton

A MEMBER OF THE HODDER HEADLINE GROUP

Acknowledgements

The front cover shows a portrait of Kaiser Wilhelm II, reproduced courtesy of Bildarchiv Preussicher Kulturbesitz, Berlin.

The publishers would like to thank the following individuals, companies and institutions for permission to reproduce copyright illustrations in this book:

Christel Gerstenberg/Corbis, page 17; Hulton-Deutsch Collection/Corbis, page 76; Punch Publications pages 26,49, 51, 65, 90 and 97.

Every effort has been made to trace and acknowledge ownership of copyright. The publishers will be happy to make arrangements with any copyright holders whom it has not been able to contact.

Orders: please contact Bookpoint Ltd, 130 Milton Park, Abingdon, Oxon OX14 4SB. Telephone (44) 01235 827720, Fax: (44) 01235 400454. Lines are open from 9.00–6.00, Monday to Saturday, with a 24 hour message answering service. Email address: orders@bookpoint.co.uk

British Library Cataloguing in Publication Data
A catalogue record for this title is available from the British Library

ISBN 0 340 804319

First published 2001
Impression number   10 9 8 7 6 5 4 3 2 1
Year   2007 2006 2005 2004 2003 2002 2001

Typeset by Fakenham Photosetting Limited, Fakenham, Norfolk
Printed in Great Britain for Hodder & Stoughton Educational, a division of Hodder Headline Plc, 338 Euston Road, London NW1 3BH by Bath Press Ltd.

Contents

Preface

To the general reader

Although the *Access to History* series has been designed with the needs of students studying the subject at higher examination levels very much in mind, it also has a great deal to offer the general reader. The main body of the text (i.e. ignoring the 'Study Guides' at the ends of chapters) forms a readable and yet stimulating survey of a coherent topic as studied by historians. However, each author's aim has not merely been to provide a clear explanation of what happened in the past (to interest and inform): it has also been assumed that most readers wish to be stimulated into thinking further about the topic and to form opinions of their own about the significance of the events that are described and discussed (to be challenged). Thus, although no prior knowledge of the topic is expected on the reader's part, she or he is treated as an intelligent and thinking person throughout. The author tends to share ideas and possibilities with the reader, rather than passing on numbers of so-called 'historical truths'.

To the student reader

Although advantage has been taken of the publication of a second edition to ensure the results of recent research are reflected in the text, the main alteration from the first edition is the inclusion of new features, and the modification of existing ones, aimed at assisting you in your study of the topic at AS level, A level and Higher. Two features are designed to assist you during your first reading of a chapter. The *Points to Consider* section following each chapter title is intended to focus your attention on the main theme(s) of the chapter, and the issues box following most section headings alerts you to the question or questions to be dealt with in the section. The *Working on . . .* section at the end of each chapter suggests ways of gaining maximum benefit from the chapter.

There are many ways in which the series can be used by students studying History at a higher level. It will, therefore, be worthwhile thinking about your own study strategy before you start your work on this book. Obviously, your strategy will vary depending on the aim you have in mind, and the time for study that is available to you.

If, for example, you want to acquire a general overview of the topic in the shortest possible time, the following approach will probably be the most effective:

1. Read chapter 1. As you do so, keep in mind the issues raised in the *Points to Consider* section.
2. Read the *Points to Consider* section at the beginning of chapter 2 and decide whether it is necessary for you to read this chapter.
3. If it is, read the chapter, stopping at each heading or sub-heading to note

down the main points that have been made. Often, the best way of doing this is to answer the question(s) posed in the Key Issues boxes.
4. Repeat stage 2 (and stage 3 where appropriate) for all the other chapters.

If, however, your aim is to gain a thorough grasp of the topic, taking however much time is necessary to do so, you may benefit from carrying out the same procedure with each chapter, as follows:

1. Try to read the chapter in one sitting. As you do this, bear in mind any advice given in the *Points to Consider* section.
2. Study the flow diagram at the end of the chapter, ensuring that you understand the general 'shape' of what you have just read.
3. Read the *Working on ...* section and decide what further work you need to do on the chapter. In particularly important sections of the book, this is likely to involve reading the chapter a second time and stopping at each heading and sub-heading to think about (and probably to write a summary of) what you have just read.
4. Attempt the *Source-based questions* section. It will sometimes be sufficient to think through your answers, but additional understanding will often be gained by forcing yourself to write them down.

When you have finished the main chapters of the book, study the 'Further Reading' section and decide what additional reading (if any) you will do on the topic.

This book has been designed to help make your studies both enjoyable and successful. If you can think of ways in which this could have been done more effectively, please contact us. In the meantime, we hope that you will gain greatly from your study of History.

Keith Randell & Robert Pearce

1 Introduction: Europe and the Great Powers

POINTS TO CONSIDER

This chapter provides an introduction to international relations after 1870. It does so by sketching in vital background information on Europe before this date and on the Franco-Prussian War of 1870–1. Most important of all, it considers each of the Great Powers in turn, looking at their politics, their economies, and the problems with which they had to grapple. The study of international relations involves far more than foreign affairs, since the foreign policy of a state is generally influenced by domestic issues. It is important that you grasp the distinctive character and aims of each country, and also that you are familiar with the sources of tension in Europe in the 1870–1914 period. A thorough understanding of this chapter will enable you to tackle the rest of the book with confidence.

KEY DATES

1866		Austro-Prussian War.
1867		The 'Dual Monarchy' of Austria-Hungary was created.
1870	July	Start of the Franco-Prussian War.
1871	Jan	German unification, end of Franco-Prussian War;
	May	Treaty of Frankfurt.
1889		Britain's Naval Defence Act.
1890		Fall of Bismarck.
1894		Franco-Russian Alliance.
1904		*Entente Cordiale* (France and Britain).
1909		Revolution by the 'Young Turks'.
1914	28 June	assassination of Franz Ferdinand, leading to the outbreak of the First World War.

1 Europe in 1870–1914

> **KEY ISSUE** Why is the 1870–1914 period of such profound historical significance?

The years from 1870 to 1914 are generally considered to be one of the most momentous periods in the history of the modern world. It was an era dominated by nationalism. It began with war, between two Great Powers, and ended with war, a bloodbath between all the Great Powers. In between there was a long period of peace and relative harmony (or 'accord'). It was a time of industrial growth and urbanisation. Yet there was still rivalry between the nations of Europe. Each state produced more and more sophisticated and destructive weapons, each believed itself superior and each subscribed to the dangerous idea that war could not be delayed indefinitely – a potentially explosive cocktail.

It was also an age of imperialism. Europeans, buoyed up with false notions of their own moral superiority, believed that they had the right to conquer and govern the undeveloped portions of the world. They certainly had a superiority in weaponry. In the 1880s and 1890s Africa was partitioned between the Great Powers. China seemed to be next, but before this could happen an assassination in the Balkans on 28 June 1914 produced the First World War. Europe would never be the same again. The war had momentous consequences, playing an important role in producing the Russian revolution, the Great Depression, the rise of Hitler, the Second World War and the decolonisation of Europe's empires. Its impact on ideas – on the way we perceive the world – was to be no less profound than its impact on power politics. Small wonder that historians are fascinated by the years from 1870 to 1914 and by the origins of the war.

2 The Franco-Prussian War, 1870–71

> **KEY ISSUE** What were the main effects of this conflict?

a) The War and the Treaty

In July 1870, the French government blundered into a conflict with Prussia. By declaring war to avenge a slight to her national honour, the French fell into a trap that the Prussian king's chief minister, Otto von Bismarck (see the Profile on page 17), had carefully laid for them. War against France, the 'traditional enemy', was Bismarck's best chance of inflaming German national feeling and persuading the independent south German states to unite with the Prussian-dominated states of the north, thereby unifying Germany.

Bismarck had decided to provoke France when he secretly pressed the claims of a distant relative of the King of Prussia to the vacant Spanish throne. To his dismay, however, the plot misfired and France scored a diplomatic victory by issuing a dignified and restrained protest. But the French government, pushed on by warlike public opinion, foolishly demanded guarantees that the Prussian claim to Spain would never be renewed. In a remarkable display of ingenuity, Bismarck edited the king's factual report of his encounter with the French ambassador to read as a deliberate insult to France. When this version – 'a red rag to the Gallic bull' as Bismarck called it – was published in the press, France's honour could only be satisfied by a declaration of war.

The Franco-Prussian war was a disaster for France. She entered the war without allies and with a badly organised army, whose slow and inefficient mobilisation put her at an immediate disadvantage compared with the speedy Prussian forces. The bulk of the French army was no match for the well-trained, highly disciplined and well-led Prussians and their German allies. The French were not only outnumbered and outgunned, they were completely outmanoeuvred.

The outcome was decided by two major encounters in the opening stages of the war. At Sedan, in early September, one French army was defeated and surrendered with over 80,000 men, including the French Emperor. At Metz, in late October, the main French army of over 150,000 men, which had been encircled for over two months, capitulated. The war continued for another three months as new armies were raised, but despite a few successes they failed to break the siege of Paris. The French capital finally fell in January 1871, after a terrible ordeal.

The peace terms, embodied in the Treaty of Frankfurt, were severe. The victors annexed Alsace and Lorraine, two provinces with rich iron ore deposits, textile industries and good agricultural land. An indemnity of 5,000 million francs was also demanded, and until it was paid German troops occupied parts of France. The final humiliation was a victory march through Paris.

France's troubles were not over with the ending of the war. Paris set itself up as a rival authority to the government. After the proclamation of a 'Commune', a socialist and workers' regime was inaugurated in late March 1871. When the Communards refused to agree to the government's terms, troops took the city by force in late May, amidst scenes of appalling ferocity.

b) The War's Consequences

The Franco-Prussian war had enormous implications for Europe, not least because it led to the unification of Germany. The King of Prussia was proclaimed German Emperor in the Hall of Mirrors at the palace of Versailles in January 1871. The incorporation of the southern states, including Bavaria and Würtemberg (though not the 10 million Germans in Austria), into the new German Empire transformed the political situation in central Europe. Instead of a relatively weak collection of states with powerful neighbours on each side, 'Germany' was now a major power. Assisted by political unity, its economy now expanded remarkably. The British politician Benjamin Disraeli remarked that this 19th-century 'German Revolution' was of even greater importance than the French Revolution of the previous century.

Military tactics would have to change, as the success of the Prussian military machine necessitated a reappraisal of conventional wisdom. Prussia's victory demonstrated the importance of a competent General Staff, capable of planning military operations and utilising railways effectively for the rapid movement of troops and supplies. Future wars, it was now widely believed, would be wars of movement and of short duration, with a premium on rapid mobilisation. Conscription was deemed necessary to provide adequate trained reserves, while the Prussian education system was hailed as contributing to the superiority of her armies over semi-literate French peasant soldiers. Preparing for war would clearly be a long-term, peacetime activity.

The emergence of a powerful German Empire upset the existing balance of power in Europe. The defeat of France marked the end of an era in which she had been regarded as the greatest military power on the continent; and Prussia's defeat of France in 1871 came hard on the heels of her victory over Austria in 1866. This left Russia as the only major military power in Europe, besides Germany. Italy also gained from the war, occupying Rome, which had hitherto been denied her by the presence of French troops defending the interests of the papacy. The defeat of France in 1870–71, therefore, helped create a new system of international relations in Europe, in which Germany was likely to play a dominant role.

3 The Great Powers of Europe

> **KEY ISSUE** How did the Great Powers differ from each other in their politics, economy and foreign policy aims?

a) Germany

From 1815 until the Austro-Prussian war of 1866, 'Germany' had not been a single country but a geographical expression, a loose confederation of 39 states of very variable size. The two most powerful of these were Austria and Prussia, who were also major Powers in their own right. Prussia began to establish economic ascendancy over Austria from the 1830s by means of the *Zollverein*, a customs union from which Austria was excluded. Then Bismarck used what he called 'blood and iron' – i.e. warfare, against Denmark, Prussia and finally France – to unify Germany. Hence he was able to control the process of unification and ensure that Prussia dominated the new state.

The German Empire of 1871 tended to be authoritarian and militaristic. Executive power (decision making) belonged to the Kaiser (Emperor) and the Chancellor (chief minister) The Chancellor and the other ministers were appointed by the Kaiser and could only be dismissed by him, not by the parliament (Reichstag). Hence the German system was very different from that of Great Britain. The Kaiser was also Supreme War Lord. Hence the military chiefs had direct access to him, bypassing the ministers. There was a Reichstag elected by universal suffrage, but this was unable to exercise much control over the government. Even so, the Imperial Chancellor needed the agreement of the Reichstag in passing laws and voting taxation and had to make strenuous efforts to secure a pro-government majority.

From 1871 to 1890, Germany was dominated by Bismarck. The old Kaiser, William I, who was already 64 when he had become King of Prussia in 1861, trusted him on most issues and his prestige as the creator of a united Germany was enormous. Bismarck was also an extremely able politician and statesman. After his dismissal in 1890, lesser figures were in charge. Policy-making was shared between the new Kaiser Wilhelm II (see the Profile on page 76), the Chancellor and the foreign minister, as well as the military and naval chiefs.

Between 1871 and 1914, Germany became the greatest industrial power in Europe. Unification, by creating a single internal market with a common currency and system of weights and measures, contributed to rapid economic expansion. German industrialisation was characterised by the growth of heavy industry (iron and steel) and the emergence of new industries (including chemicals), as well as by rapid urbanisation.

This industrialisation was significant in several ways. By 1914 Germany had outstripped its European rivals (see the table on page 6), and was second in the world only to the United States. The growth of the German economy intensified the competition amongst industrial states for markets and raw materials. This, combined with population growth, increased the pressure for overseas colonies. Within Germany, it generated considerable social tension, as the working and middle classes challenged the dominance of the traditional land-owning Prussian aristocracy (Junkers). How might the government defuse these tensions? Constitutional reform – giving power to middle-class or working-class political parties – was refused outright. But perhaps foreign policy might distract attention from internal problems. In the Bismarckian decades, it is said, colonial policy was to serve this purpose – hence the term 'social imperialism'. Under Wilhelm II, overseas policy in general (*Weltpolitik*) was used for the same ends.

Many feared that the newly unified Germany would seek to translate its economic power into dominance over other states. In fact Bismarck regarded Germany as a 'satisfied' Power, and yet he needed the prestige from success in international affairs to bolster his position at home. Would he – and his successors – seek to follow the traditional Prussian policy of co-operation with the conservative powers of Austria-Hungary and Russia, or might he seek an alliance with Great Britain? Would the 'Anglo-Saxon' nations of Germany and Britain be partners or rivals? Certainly it was on Germany, geographically midway between the other Great Powers in Europe, that would fall a good deal of the responsibility for producing peace or war.

The Great Powers of Europe		
	Population	Iron & Steel Output (tonnes)
Germany	49 m. in 1890 66 m. in 1914	4 m. in 1890 18 m. in 1914
France	38 m. in 1890 40 m. in 1914	2 m. in 1890 5 m. in 1915
Great Britain	37 m. in 1890 46 m. in 1914	8 m. in 1890 8 m. in 1914
Austria-Hungary	42 m. in 1890 52 m. in 1914	1 m. in 1890 3 m. in 1914
Russia	116 m. in 1890 175 m. in 1914	1 m. in 1890 5 m. in 1914

b) France

French power in Europe had been at its height under Napoleon, when France was the wealthiest and, barring Russia, the most populous nation on the continent. For many years after his defeat in 1815, France continued to be regarded as a threat to peace. Partly this was due to her reputation as a military nation, partly to her reputation as the home of revolutionary ideas, a view that was reinforced by the revolutions of 1830 and 1848, which spread from France to other parts of Europe. Yet from 1815 to 1852 France pursued a largely peaceful foreign policy. The real challenge to the existing European order came with the reign of Napoleon III (nephew of the great Napoleon) from 1852 to 1870.

During this period, France – in the 'Crimean Coalition' with Britain – defeated Russia in 1854. French armies also fought in north Italy in 1859 in the 'war of liberation', directed against Austria – a sign of Louis Napoleon's sympathy for the cause of 'nationality'. The same support for nationalism led France to stay neutral when Prussia fought Austria in 1866, enabling Prussia to unite the north German states. Yet in 1870–71 France paid the price for Napoleon's miscalculation in fostering the growth of Prussian power.

France made a rapid recovery from her defeat in the early 1870s. She paid off the indemnity demanded by the Treaty of Frankfurt within a few years and regained her status as a Great Power. Her reorganised army, now based on compulsory military service, came to be regarded as an effective military force. She also developed a fairly powerful navy.

Yet while the Franco-Prussian war had been regarded as a war between equals, in 1914 there were great differences between the two states in both population and industrial strength. France's industrialisation was slower, more spasmodic and less complete than Germany's. This showed most obviously in output of coal and iron and steel, but also in the higher proportion of her population still engaged in farming. The French rate of population increase was much less than Germany's and lower than that of all the other Great Powers. Nevertheless, France remained a very wealthy country. Vast amounts of capital were invested abroad, especially in Russia.

Politically, the contrast between France and Germany was also striking. The Third Republic was undoubtedly democratic, but executive power was weak. Governments were usually short-lived, and this made it difficult to maintain a consistent foreign policy. It also meant that governments had trouble keeping control over enthusiasts for imperial expansion.

France was a very divided society. By 1900 the French Left (Socialists and Radicals) was largely pacifist and anti-militarist in outlook. On the other hand, a vocal section of the French Right had become very nationalistic and committed to *revanche* (revenge, against Germany for defeat in 1871 and the loss of Alsace-Lorraine). The influence of the idea of *revanche* on the policies of French governments can easily be exaggerated. Nevertheless, it persisted as an ideal – something that should not be forgotten – for many Frenchmen.

In the 1870s French foreign policy reverted to the tradition of the liberal alliance with Britain. In the following decade, however, colonial rivalries soured Anglo-French relations, especially in Africa. France herself became a great imperial power in this period with extensive colonial possessions in Africa and Asia. Hence the French republic turned to the monarchical state of Russia. An alliance with Russia, completed in 1894, became the keystone of French foreign policy and her guarantee of security against an increasingly powerful Germany. In practice, however, the alliance seemed to be anti-British in its direction until 1904, when France reached a colonial agreement with Britain. This began as merely a friendly relationship (*Entente Cordiale*), but demonstrations of German hostility towards France between 1905 and 1911 gradually converted it, by 1914, into something approaching a military alliance between France and Britain.

c) Great Britain

Britain was one of the leading Great Powers in 1815, having contributed substantially to the defeat of Napoleon; and for the next half-century Britain continued to play a prominent role in international affairs, participating in diplomatic conferences (the 'Concert of Europe') through which the Powers tried to resolve major problems by negotiation rather than war.

A major influence on British foreign policy was suspicion of

Russia's designs on Constantinople, the capital of the Ottoman Empire, and possibly on Britain's possessions in India. It was feared that if Russia occupied Constantinople, she would be able to dominate the Near East. British ministers therefore supported the declining Ottoman Empire as a buffer against Russian expansion. The Crimean War of 1854–56 was fought mainly to check Russian influence over Turkey. But Britain became disillusioned, having made heavy sacrifices for meagre results, and turned against active involvement in European conflicts. This mood, combined with suspicion of Napoleon III's motives, largely explains why Britain was mainly a passive spectator of Bismarck's three wars in the 1860s.

The recovery of world trade in the 1850s also tended to divert British attention away from Europe towards more distant parts of the world. As the 'first industrial nation', Britain enjoyed many advantages over her continental rivals for several decades, enabling her to expand her trade worldwide.

Between 1870 and 1914, Britain became the greatest imperial power in the world. With colonial possessions scattered across the globe, hers was 'the empire on which the sun never set'. She was losing her pre-eminence as a manufacturing nation, being overtaken by the USA and Germany, but still relied on imported food and raw materials and on overseas markets for the sale of her manufactured goods. The nation's lifeblood was the uninterrupted flow of seaborne trade, and therefore Britain needed to 'rule the waves' and to defend the sea lanes with her navy. Fears that her fleet was inadequate for the country's needs led to the Naval Defence Act of 1889, which established the principle of the 'Two Power Standard': the Royal Navy was to be as large as the combined fleets of the next two naval powers. It came as a shock to Britons when, from 1898, Germany began to construct a large fleet. The army played a far less conspicuous role, and Britain was the only European Power that did not introduce conscription after 1871.

Britain had a well-established parliamentary system of government, which was democratised by stages in the nineteenth century. The monarch reigned but did not rule; and the aristocracy, though still having a very prominent role, shared power and influence with the prosperous middle class. This was a more 'open' society than in Germany, in which people of ability could rise to the top. One important difference between the two systems was the simple fact that in Britain the government of the day had to command a majority in parliament (especially in the House of Commons) to continue in office. Governments therefore took careful note of the views of MPs as well as of the press, and so were, to some extent, more responsive to the needs of the public.

British foreign policy naturally reflected, in part, her interests as a commercial and imperial nation. Immense importance was attached to safeguarding the routes to India, so that the Suez canal and southern Africa were regarded as areas of strategic concern. The defence of India itself, threatened by Russia's expansion into Central Asia, was also a major anxiety. Since the navy was incapable of sailing up the Khyber Pass, the retort to a Russian threat to India was to consider sending a fleet into the Black Sea, to threaten Russia's vulnerable southern coastline.

Traditionally, Britain also had been concerned to prevent any one Power from dominating the European continent, but from the mid-1860s to about 1900 the balance of power in Europe was not an important influence on British policy. This was the period of so-called 'Splendid Isolation', when Britain stood aside from alliances on the continent. Nevertheless, Britain continued to be involved in European affairs, especially those relating to the Ottoman Empire and the Straits – the strategic waterway linking the Mediterranean and the Black Sea. By the turn of the century, however, many British statesmen were becoming convinced that Britain's resources were overstretched and that she needed allies if she were to maintain her role as a world power.

d) Austria-Hungary

From 1815 to 1848, the Austrian Chancellor, Metternich, had exercised great influence in Europe, working closely with Russia and Prussia in an informal conservative alliance opposed to revolutionary movements. After this period, however, important changes occurred which lessened Austria's power and prestige. Economically, she declined relative to the other Great Powers. Indeed her economic progress was dwarfed by that of other countries. In foreign policy she gave diplomatic support, in 1854, to Britain and France in the Crimean War, thus alienating her former ally Russia. Then she suffered defeats in wars of national unification, in north Italy in 1859 and against Prussia in 1866. She was becoming increasingly unable to play a fully independent role in international affairs.

Austria was in some ways an anachronism: in an age of growing nationalism (when each separate national group demanded its own nation state), she was the property of the Habsburg dynasty and contained many different national groups. In 1867 an important change occurred. The Habsburgs compromised with the Hungarians (or Magyars) by granting them self-government. 'Austria' became 'Austria-Hungary', sometimes called the 'Dual Monarchy': Austria had its capital at Vienna, and Hungary its own government and parliament at Budapest. There was to be a common foreign policy and a uniform army, but in most other matters the two states were separate.

There were now two 'master races' in the Austro-Hungarian Empire, the Germans in the West and the Magyars in the East. But there were also numerous other races: Czechs, Slovaks, Poles, Italians, Serbs, Croats and others. These were 'subject races', and they were discriminated against by the Germans and Magyars. The scale of the problem can be seen from the fact that mobilisation posters had to be printed in 15 separate languages! The Emperor, Franz Joseph, was popular and well-intentioned, but conflicts between the nationalities were endless. Concessions to one group only provoked protests or riots by another. In Hungary, the dominant Magyars ignored the claims of 'inferior' peoples and so alienated the traditionally loyal Croats, as well as the Serbs. The result was a Serbo-Croat alliance within Austria-Hungary that looked beyond the borders of the state to the independent Balkan kingdom of Serbia as a means of escape from Magyar oppression. The 'south Slav' problem, as it was called, soon threatened Austria-Hungary with disintegration.

By 1871, the Austro-Hungarian government regarded the Balkans as a vital sphere of political influence and economic activity. This raised the problem of whether to oppose Russia or co-operate with her in Balkan issues. In 1871 Austria-Hungary hoped for an anti-Russian alliance with Germany, but this conflicted with Bismarck's desire for good relations with Russia. In order to check Russian influence, therefore, Austrian policy was directed towards creating client states in the Balkans and propping up the imperial power there, the Ottoman Empire. Co-operation with Britain in the area was another option, and this served Austria-Hungary well for a time. Yet the growth of nationalism in the Balkan states, particularly after 1900, raised serious problems. The most serious threat came from the independent Balkan state of Serbia, especially since Serbia was backed by Russia.

e) Russia

Tsarist Russia was a powerful force in European affairs in the first half of the nineteenth century. Her aim was to defend monarchical authority. After the upheavals of 1848, the Tsarist regime – the only sizeable continental state impervious to the revolutionary fever – was again determined to act as a stabilising, conservative force.

Then came defeat in the Crimean War of 1854–56, a shattering blow to Russian prestige. It was a source of deep humiliation to the Tsar that Russia was now forbidden to maintain a navy in the Black Sea or to garrison a naval base on its shores. Internally, it inspired an attempt to modernise local government, the army and educational system, and brought about the abolition of serfdom in 1861. The effect on Russian foreign policy was equally dramatic. From being the defender of the existing state of affairs (the *status quo*), Russia became a 'revisionist' Power. She repaid Austria's 'treachery' in siding with the western powers in 1854 by remaining neutral when Napoleon III, and later Bismarck, fought the Austrian Empire in 1859 and 1866. In 1870, during the Franco-Prussian war, the Tsar insisted that he would not be bound by the hated 'Black Sea clauses'.

Russia was both a European and an Asiatic power. Enormous in extent, with a population (in European Russia alone) equal to that of Germany and Austria-Hungary combined, Russia was making great strides towards overcoming her backwardness compared with the other Great Powers. Rapid industrialisation in the 1890s yielded the highest annual rate of increase in industrial production in the world and produced an impressive expansion of heavy industry and of the railway network. Russia was acquiring many of the trappings of a modern state.

Yet Russia was a colossus with feet of clay, as her defeat by Japan in the war of 1904–5 was to demonstrate. A number of serious weaknesses prevented her from realising her full potential as a Great Power.

Firstly, the Russian economy did not generate enough taxable wealth to meet the increasing needs of the state. Russian agriculture remained generally unproductive but grain from the richer regions had to be exported to pay for imported machinery for her industries. Industrialisation was also partly financed by massive foreign loans, which increased the size of the state debt. If the peacetime army and navy was a heavy burden on the treasury, war itself was a luxury Russia could not afford. The war with Japan virtually bankrupted the state.

Secondly, the persistence of widespread social and political discontent weakened the fabric of the state. Finally, the government was incompetent. The Tsars clung to their autocratic powers, insisting on their divine mission, but they were quite incapable of ruling effectively. When a parliament, the *Duma*, was eventually permitted in 1905, it had little power to influence the government. On top of this, the Russian bureaucracy was notoriously corrupt and incompetent. It is hardly surprising, therefore, that Russia was not the great military Power that her size and resources suggested. Nor was it a coincidence that defeat was followed by revolution in 1905.

The formation of a united Germany in 1871, altering the political situation in Central Europe and creating a powerful neighbour on her western frontier, caused Russia considerable concern. In the Bismarck era (1871–90), Russia was content to work in association or alliance with Germany. The non-renewal of the alliance after Bismarck's fall led to an alliance with France, as a guarantee of security, though it was not always a close or harmonious alliance.

Russian policy towards the Ottoman Empire was a curious mixture of practical politics and romanticism. Control of the Straits, linking the Black Sea with the Mediterranean, was vital for Russian trade and her status as a European Power. The idea of recovering Constantinople from the Turks, on the other hand, was a dream that had excited the Russian imagination for over a century. However impracticable, the idea still influenced Russian policy at various times.

The official policy, pursued by the foreign ministry, was a cautious one, recognising that the 'Eastern Question' was a matter of concern to all the Great Powers. Russia would simply try to exploit favourable situations to secure advantages for herself or her client stages in the Balkans. 'Pan-Slavists', however, accepted no such restraints. They believed in the solidarity of all Slavs, whether in Russia itself or the Balkans. To them, Russia's mission was to liberate the Balkan Christians from Turkish oppression; and they wished to create independent Slav states under the protection of Mother Russia and the Orthodox Church.

A clash between Russia and Austria-Hungary over the Balkans was virtually certain. Russia was encouraging Slav nationalism. But the results of this would be the creation of new Balkan states and even – if these states proved attractive enough to Austria-Hungary's subject races – the disintegration of the Austro-Hungarian Empire. Britain would also intervene if Russia was seen to have designs on the Straits or Constantinople. A new factor in the 1890s was the growth of German influence in Turkey as part of her economic penetration into the Near East. The Balkans were therefore the 'tinderbox' or 'powder-keg' of Europe. Or could the conflicting ambitions of the Great Powers be kept in check by the survival of the Ottoman Empire, 'the great shock-absorber of the European states system'? But how much longer could she survive?

4 The Eastern Question

> **KEY ISSUES** What useful functions were served by Turkish rule in the Balkans? Why, early in the 20th century, was that rule unlikely to survive for long?

The Ottoman Empire had once been a great military empire. Only partly European, it was a multi-national institution stretching from the borders of Austria-Hungary and Russia through the Balkans into Asia Minor, Persia and Arabia and through Egypt along the coast of north Africa (see the map on page 13). Yet by 1870, the Sultan's authority in many parts of his empire was very weak. The integration of Turks, Slavs and others in European Turkey had never been systematically attempted. The races and religions, Muslim and Christian, simply co-existed, usually in a state of mutual animosity, until grievances provoked (often very bloody) uprisings. The Ottoman Empire was in fact 'the Sick Man of Europe'. When would it die?

Throughout the nineteenth century, the 'Eastern Question' – the problems arising from the expectation that, as a British minister expressed it in 1830, 'this clumsy fabric of barbarous power will speedily crumble into pieces from its own inherent causes of decay' – caused a series of crises in international affairs. The decline, or possible disintegration, of the Ottoman Empire carried with it the danger of conflict amongst the Great Powers.

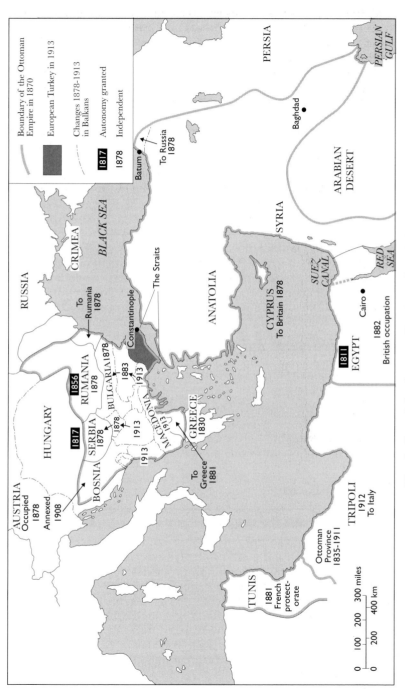

The decline of the Ottoman Empire, 1870–1913.

Legend:
- Boundary of the Ottoman Empire in 1870
- European Turkey in 1913
- Changes 1878–1913 in Balkans
- Autonomy granted
- 1817 Independent
- 1878

PERSIA

PERSIAN GULF

Baghdad

ARABIAN DESERT

BLACK SEA

CRIMEA

Batum
To Russia 1878

RUSSIA

To Rumania 1878

SYRIA

The Straits

Constantinople

ANATOLIA

RED SEA

SUEZ CANAL

CYPRUS
To Britain 1878

1811 EGYPT
Cairo
1882
British occupation

HUNGARY

AUSTRIA
Occupied 1878
Annexed 1908

1856 RUMANIA 1878

1817 SERBIA 1878

BOSNIA

BULGARIA 1878
1883
1913

1878
1913

MACEDONIA 1913

1913

GREECE 1830

To Greece 1881

TRIPOLI
1912
To Italy

Ottoman Province 1835–1911

TUNIS
1881
French protectorate

0   100   200   300 miles
0   200   400 km

There was no simple solution to the Easter Question in the period from 1871 to 1914. Partition of the Turkish Empire would probably result in war, since there was little hope of agreement on how to divide it among the Powers. An alternative was to assist the Balkan states to obtain autonomy (self-government) or even complete independence from Turkey, as Greece, Serbia, Montenegro and Rumania had done earlier in the century. This solution was favoured by Russia, but opposed by Austria-Hungary. British governments also doubted the wisdom of weakening Turkey's ability to act as a barrier to Russian expansion. The only other alternative was to 'prop-up' the Ottoman Empire in order to postpone its collapse, while putting pressure on the Turkish government to introduce reforms to improve the lot of its Christian subjects. This was the policy favoured by the majority of the Powers.

In fact, Turkish sovereignty over European Turkey had been steadily eroded for over a century by the Great Powers, who claimed rights of protection over their co-religionists or special privileges for their resident nationals. Throughout the nineteenth century, the Turkish economy was subjected to increasing exploitation by European commercial groups, backed by their governments, who secured concessions for mining, manufacturing or transport facilities. Furthermore, in 1881, the Europeans set up an agency to supervise the Turkish finances, following a declaration of bankruptcy.

Widespread resentment amongst the Muslim population at this sort of European interference led to a dramatic change in government. In 1909 the Sultan was overthrown by a revolution of the 'Young Turks'. Their aim was to rejuvenate the empire by modernising the country and creating a more liberal form of government. Yet only a few years later the Balkan states joined together and inflicted a crushing defeat on the Turkish army. By 1913, European Turkey had been reduced to a mere fraction of its former size.

5 Conclusion

> **KEY ISSUE** What is the significance of the 1870–1914 period?

1870–1914 started and ended with war, and the years between the wars saw significant problems and rivalries. There was friction between France and Germany, stemming from the Franco-Prussian War. There were also fundamental disagreements between Austria-Hungary and Russia over the solution to the problems posed by the decline of Ottoman power in the Balkans. We can clearly see that the ingredients that produced the First World War were generated in these years, especially if we add Britain's naval rivalry with Germany to the brew.

Yet if the pre-conditions for war were created in these years, we should not be deluded into thinking that the war which broke out in 1914 was in any sense inevitable. After all, the same factors which led to war in 1914 had produced peace in the previous decades. The fact is that there were over 40 years of peace in Europe after 1871, and we do scant justice to this period of history if we see it merely as a prelude to the Great War. In order to understand rivalry and accord between the Powers we have to investigate the period in depth.

Working on Chapter I

It is more important to grasp the broad issues in this chapter than to write detailed notes. In particular, you need to understand the basic issues involved in the 'Eastern Question'. It was said that if the Ottoman Empire did not exist, it would be necessary to invent her, so many useful purposes did she serve. Can you explain this? You also need to identify the strengths and weaknesses of each Great Power, and to note the particular issues or regions which were of concern to them.

Summary diagram
Europe and the Great Powers

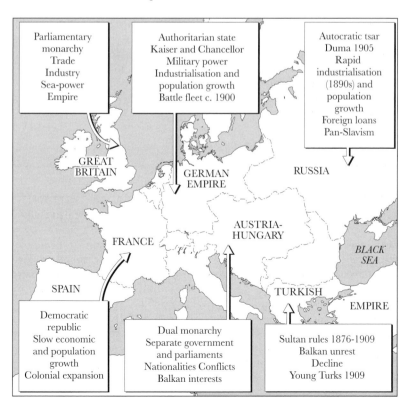

2 Bismarck and Europe, 1871–90

POINTS TO CONSIDER

This chapter considers the long period of European diplomacy when Bismarck, Germany's Chancellor, dominated affairs. It is important to be aware of what he actually did (for instance, the alliances that he made), in the context of the problems that beset Europe. It is also necessary to try to assess his motives and estimate the results of his actions – issues that have attracted very different verdicts from historians. You also need to grapple with the 'success' or 'failure' of his policies, and to be aware of what is meant by these slippery and deceptively simple terms.

KEY DATES

1873	Three Emperors' League, between Germany, Austria-Hungary and Russia.
1875	'War in Sight' Crisis.
1875–8	Balkan Crisis.
1878	The Congress of Berlin.
1879	The Dual Alliance (Germany and Austria-Hungary).
1881	Three Emperors' Alliance.
1882	The Triple Alliance (Germany, Austria-Hungary and Italy).
1887	Reinsurance Treaty (Germany and Russia); Mediterranean Agreements (Britain, Italy and Austria-Hungary).
1888	Wilhelm II becomes Kaiser.
1890	Bismarck's fall.

1 1871–75

> **KEY ISSUE** What were Bismarck's aims in foreign policy?

Germany's triumph over France in 1871, following her earlier victories over Denmark and Austria, made her the greatest military Power on the continent. It also upset the existing balance of power in Europe. There was consequently considerable fear and suspicion that the new German Empire might continue to pursue an aggressive foreign policy. Bismarck, however, harboured no further expansionist designs. In his view, Germany was now a satisfied, or 'satiated', Power. He dismissed any further conquest as 'folly beyond all political reason'. He had achieved his aim of a Prussian-dominated German state; his main objective now was the security of the German Empire. The best guarantee of this was European peace.

OTTO VON BISMARCK (1815–1898)

-Profile-

A conservative and a royalist, from a Prussian Junker family, Bismarck entered politics in 1847 as a member of the Prussian Diet. From 1859 he was Prussian ambassador in St Petersburg and then Paris, but in 1862 he was recalled during a constitutional crisis. The Prussian Reichstag was refusing to vote money for army reforms, and the King, Wilhelm I, considered either abdicating in favour of his liberal son or using the army to dissolve the Reichstag. Instead, he decided to make Bismarck, who had the reputation of an extreme royalist, his prime minister. Bismarck collected taxation without parliamentary approval. 'The great issues of the day', he announced, would be decided not by the rigmarole of parliamentary procedure, but by 'blood and iron'.

He won over Prussia's elected representatives by unifying Germany, first the north (1866) and then (in 1871) the whole of 'Lesser Germany' (which did not include the 10 million Germans in Austria). He unified Germany because he thought unification was inevitable sooner or later. By achieving it himself, he could control the process and make sure that the new state was dominated by Prussia, whose king became Emperor (Kaiser) – and by himself. He could mastermind a revoluton 'from above', whereas a revolution 'from below' might get out of hand. He dominated German affairs for the next two decades, becoming indispensable to Wilhelm I.

In domestic affairs he had the task of securing a majority for his measures in the Reichstag. He did this by allying with particular groups, while persecuting others. His first 'enemy' was the Catholic community, and then, after 1879, the socialists. He was never defeated in the Reichstag. His fall came, ironically, because he had preserved the right of the monarch to dismiss his ministers. In 1890 Bismarck was dismissed by the young Kaiser Wilhelm II. One Liberal sensed that worse was to come, commenting that 'it is unfortunate that his departure is unfortunate'. Bismarck retired with an ill grace. He even spoke in favour of republicanism: kings, he said, were dangerous if they had real power.

In office Bismarck's aims were conservative, but he sometimes used radical measures – for instance, a progressive scheme of social reform – to prevent revolution and preserve as much as possible. He fostered change to prevent still greater change. He has been depicted as the 'sorcerer's apprentice', unleashing forces in Germany that he was unable to control, especially nationalism and imperialism. Yet he managed to preserve a semi-autocratic system of government in Germany even when, in many other countries, industrialisation was leading to a more democratic form of politics.

The two obvious threats to peace were a French war of revenge and an Austro-Russian conflict arising in the Balkans. France without allies did not pose a serious danger: Bismarck was confident that the German army could defeat her again, if necessary. But Germany's position in Europe, sandwiched between France in the west and Russia in the east, made her peculiarly vulnerable to a war on two fronts. It was the possibility of a coalition between France and either Russia or Austria-Hungary that constituted the gravest menace to Germany's security.

Bismarck's solution to the two-fold problem was to try to isolate France and to reduce friction between Austria-Hungary and Russia over the Balkans, where their interests were often at variance. In practice, this meant that he encouraged the other Great Powers (France excepted) to feel dependent on Germany's goodwill and sought to neutralise their antagonisms by a 'balancing of discontents'. Bismarck's objective, however, was not to eliminate these problems – that would have the undesirable effect of making the other Powers independent of Germany and even free to conspire against her. Bismarck's diplomacy was consequently something of a delicate balancing act: he wished to keep rivalries simmering but to prevent them boiling over.

In 1871 Bismarck's immediate concern was to reassure the leaders of Europe that he was now genuinely a man of peace. Assurances to this effect, made through normal diplomatic channels, were reinforced by personal contacts between the German Kaiser, the Habsburg Emperor and the Tsar of Russia in the summer of 1871. The outcome of these monarchical gatherings was the Three Emperors' League (*Dreikaiserbund*) of October 1873, initially an Austro-Russian treaty to which the Kaiser later gave his adherence. Although this Agreement was not of Bismarck's making, it suited his purposes well enough.

The content of the *Dreikaiserbund* of 1873 was somewhat vague. It expressed the desire of the three Emperors to stand together in the interests of monarchical solidarity against the threats of republicanism and socialism. They also wished to reduce the risks of war arising from Austro-Russian differences. Hence the promise 'to consult together so that these divergences do not take precedence over considerations of a higher order' – that is, peace and stability.

In 1875, however, Bismarck's strategy of quietly allaying fears about Germany's dominant position in Europe was suddenly discarded in a crisis with France which he himself provoked. In April the *Berlin Post* published an article (regarded as government-inspired) under the dramatic heading: 'Is War in Sight?' Contemporaries, as well as later historians, were puzzled by this incident. It seemed that Bismarck was raising the spectre of war – but for no good reason and with no clear purpose. Perhaps he was genuinely anxious at France's surprisingly rapid recovery from her defeat in 1871. Certainly the German General Staff was concerned about the newly reorganised and strengthened French army and began to talk of the need for a preventive war.

Bismarck himself seems to have calculated that a diplomatic warning would be enough to discourage the French from further military expansion, but his methods were remarkably clumsy. The crisis backfired when France secured promises of support from Britain and Russia against German threats. The 'War in Sight' crisis demonstrates that Bismarck was slow to adapt his diplomatic methods to suit Germany's dominant position in Europe, which required her leaders to act with restraint.

2 The Near East Crisis, 1875–8

> **KEY ISSUE** Why did events in the Balkans lead to a crisis between the Great Powers?

The Eastern Crisis began in 1875 with a rising against Turkish misgovernment in Bosnia and Herzegovina (see the map on page 23). The long-standing animosity of Christian peasants towards the oppressive rule of Muslim landowners was heightened by grievances over taxation and labour services. In 1876, the revolt spread to Bulgaria, then part of the Ottoman Empire, supported by the semi-independent states of Serbia and Montenegro.

The re-opening of the Eastern Question presented Bismarck with a major test of his statesmanship. Determined to avoid taking sides between his *Dreikaiserbund* partners, he had somehow to convince both Vienna and St Petersburg of Germany's goodwill. If he failed, either Austria-Hungary or Russia might seek support from France. There was no simple solution to the problem of conflicting Austro-Russian interests in the Balkans. From the Austrian point of view, the main danger lay in Russian encouragement of Slav nationalism. This was not only a threat to the integrity of the Ottoman Empire, in whose survival Austria-Hungary had a vested interest, but it also threatened the stability of the multi-national Habsburg Empire. In the case of Russia, the temptation to 'fish in trouble waters' in the hope of weakening Turkey was hard to resist. In addition, Russia, as the leader of the Orthodox Church, was under a moral obligation to aid the Christian Slavs if their Muslim Turkish rulers treated them too oppressively. Germany had good reason to be anxious at this crisis in Austro-Russian relations.

Bismarck's options were limited. He himself was prepared to contemplate the partition of the Ottoman Empire, but that was an option neither Austria-Hungary nor Russia was willing to accept. If he threw his weight behind Austria, Russia might then be driven into the arms of France. On the other hand, if he supported Russia, this might well boost Slav nationalism and lead to the break up of the Austro-Hungarian Empire. Hence he at first adopted a 'low profile' approach, encouraging the Austrians and Russians to find an agreed solution.

At this stage both Austria and Russia were sticking to the spirit of the *Dreikaiserbund*. Admittedly each side sought to extract some advantage for themselves from the situation, but neither wanted to accelerate the collapse of the Ottoman Empire. Gorchakov, the ageing and conservative Russian foreign minister, recognised that Turkey's fate concerned all the Great Powers and favoured restraint. Andrassy, his opposite number in Austria-Hungary, aware that German support was unlikely in the event of a clash with Russia, attempted to collaborate with the Russians. Their willingness to search for a solution was a great relief to Bismarck. The German Chancellor also encouraged Britain to play an active role in opposing Russia. 'England should entirely take the lead in the Eastern question,' Bismarck suggested, so as to reduce tension between his partners in the *Dreikaiserbund*. It was a role which Britain was willing enough to fill, due to her traditional suspicion of Russian designs on the Balkans and Constantinople. Nevertheless the Great Powers failed to find a diplomatic solution.

In 1876 a new, and more ferocious, stage was reached in the crisis. The 'Bulgarian Atrocities' changed the situation: the Turks allegedly massacred over 10,000 Bulgarians. Public opinion was stirred in Britain and also in Russia. In Britain, the Liberals' campaign against the 'unspeakable Turk' temporarily prevented the Conservative government under Disraeli from pursuing the traditional British policy of supporting Turkey against Russia. In Russia, the sufferings of the Balkan Christians enflamed Pan-Slavist sentiment to such an extent that the Tsarist government found itself under increasing pressure to intervene on the side of the Balkan rebels.

By the spring of 1877 Russia's patience was exhausted. Opinion in Russia had become increasingly restive as Serbs and Montenegrins faced defeat and Bulgars were subjected to ferocious reprisals by the Turks. At the news of the worsening plight of the Balkan Christians, 'Slavomania' spread throughout Russia. By 1877, several thousand

Russian volunteers were fighting in Serbia, financed by a host of Slavic Committees. The Tsar's government was openly reproached by both the press and the clergy for failing in its 'holy duty' to aid the Christian Slavs.

Yet with its finances in disorder after bad harvests and a severe depression, the Tsarist government still hesitated to declare war. In negotiations in the spring of 1877, the Austrians had only agreed to remain neutral in a Russo-Turkish war if their Balkan interests were fully respected. Worse still, Britain made it plain that she would not tolerate sweeping Russian gains at Turkey's expense. Yet Turkish intransigence seemed to leave the Tsar's government little choice. As the war minister remarked: 'Russian honour forbids us to stand about any longer with lowered guns just for the sake of peace'.

When Serbia was defeated by the Turks, the Russians felt obliged to intervene. They declared war on Turkey in April 1877, but their progress was held up by the skilful Turkish defence of the fortress of Plevna. This had two significant consequences: firstly, it deprived the Russians of the chance of a quick victory; secondly, it caused British opinion to swing back in favour of the 'heroic little Turks'. Nevertheless, the Russians were able to resume their advance on Constantinople in January 1878. In the following month the Turks sued for peace and secured an armistice. Russia had undoubtedly won the war, but she proceeded to lose the peace. Intoxicated by success and Pan-Slavist enthusiasm, the Russian government extracted severe terms from Turkey in the Treaty of San Stephano in March 1878. European Turkey was to be reduced to small unconnected territories by the creation of a Greater Bulgaria, under Russian occupation for two years, while Russia herself made some useful territorial gains.

These terms confirmed the worst fears of Andrassy, Austria's foreign minister. 'The Russians have played us false,' he complained. The attitude of Germany and Britain was crucial in persuading the Russians to revise the peace treaty. Bismarck, however, had previously declared in December 1876 that German interests in the Balkans were not 'worth the healthy bones of a single Pomeranian musketeer', and in February 1878 he had offered his services as an 'honest broker', implying that he would not take sides in the dispute. The British attitude to the situation was much more positive. Troops were summoned from India and the fleet was despatched to Turkish waters, ready to sail into the Black Sea. Faced with Austro-British hostility and the threat of war, Russia agreed to a revision of the peace terms at an international conference to be held in Berlin in the summer of 1878.

3 The Congress of Berlin

> **KEY ISSUE** What was achieved by the Berlin Treaty of 1878?

a) The Terms of the Settlement

Before the Congress met, much useful preparatory work had been done. The Russians agreed to the reduction of Greater Bulgaria in return for gains elsewhere. The Sultan promised to introduce reforms within the Ottoman Empire and to cede Cyprus to Britain, in exchange for a guarantee of his dominions in Turkey-in-Asia. Britain also agreed to back Austria-Hungary's claim to occupy Bosnia. Despite these preliminary accords, the Congress of the Great Powers which met in Berlin in June–July 1878 was not all plain sailing.

The most contentious issue was the division of Greater Bulgaria. The Russian attempt to resist its partition (despite their earlier agreement) clashed with Britain's determination to limit the size of a Russian-dominated state. The Russian delegates only gave way when Disraeli resorted to the novel expedient of ordering his special train to be ready to leave Berlin at a few hours' notice. As a result, Greater Bulgaria was divided into three (see the map on page 23). The northern part, Bulgaria, was granted complete independence, under Russian supervision. To the south, a province named Eastern Rumelia – to emphasise its separate existence – was to have a form of self-government under Turkish control. The third part, called Macedonia, was returned to Turkish rule (or misrule).

A number of other issues were decided in favour of the interests of the Great Powers. Russia recovered Bessarabia, which she had lost to Rumania in 1856 after the Crimean War. She also acquired Batum, a valuable port on the eastern edge of the Black Sea, from Turkey. The Turks objected strongly to the loss of Bosnia to the Austrians and were reluctant to cede Cyprus to Britain, but their protests were ignored. Russian objections were also ignored when Britain claimed the right (with the Sultan's assent) to send warships into the Black Sea whenever she judged it necessary. France, who had played a minor role during the crisis, made no territorial gains in 1878 but was encouraged to seek compensation in Tunisia – still under the nominal control of the Sultan of Turkey.

The Congress of Berlin reasserted the concept that the fate of Turkey was a matter of concern to all the Great Powers and could not be decided unilaterally, as Russia had attempted to do in the Treaty of San Stephano, now described by one Russian diplomat as 'the greatest act of stupidity that we could have committed'.

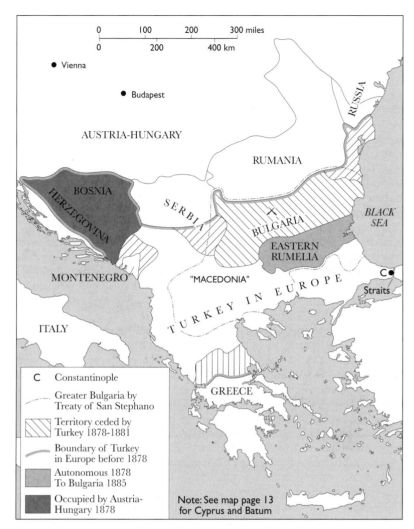

The Balkans (1878–81) and the Congress of Berlin.

b) The Significance of the Settlement

Most historians regard the Treaty of Berlin as only a temporary and limited solution of the Eastern Question. On the positive side, it can be said to have checked Russian domination of the Balkans, and without a war amongst the Great Powers. The Sultan was also obliged to treat his Christian subjects more gently – for a time, at least. This apart, it is hard to see what the Congress really 'settled'. The separation of Eastern Rumelia from Bulgaria was reversed within a decade, causing another crisis amongst the powers in 1885–88; and

Macedonia, restored to Turkish rule, became a source of constant unrest in later decades. Austrian rule in Bosnia had to be enforced by military action and was bitterly resented by both Turks and Serbs. The outright annexation of the province in 1908 also caused a major crisis. The Sultan evaded implementing serious reforms in Asia Minor, which was the scene of new massacres in the 1890s. 'A rickety sort of Turkish rule', as Salisbury, the new British foreign secretary, called it, had been re-established in 1878 even though, as he admitted, 'it is a mere respite; there is no vitality left in them'. Nevertheless, the Ottoman Empire survived for another 40 years.

What were the alternatives? One was to allow Russia to dominate the Balkans. Another was to have put more faith in the ability of the Balkan peoples, especially the Bulgarians, to govern themselves. This was Salisbury's view when he subsequently remarked that 'we backed the wrong horse'. Some historians suggest that the Great Powers' neglect of the ambitions and claims of the smaller Balkan states was a fundamental defect of the Treaty of Berlin. Although Serbia, Rumania and Montenegro became fully independent states, their territorial gains were quite small. In short, the great weakness of the Berlin settlement was that it shelved, rather than solved, most of the problems that it dealt with.

Bismarck was not to blame for this. In the course of the crisis he had advocated partition of the Ottoman Empire as the best solution. He favoured an east-west division of the Balkans between Russia and Austria-Hungary. In addition, Britain was to take Egypt, while France should have Tunisia. When this failed, his main concern was to ensure that Britain, not Austria-Hungary, took the lead in opposing Russia. Although he performed well enough in his role of 'honest broker' at the Congress of Berlin, the Russians showed little gratitude for the support he gave to their interests.

The Congress of Berlin was certainly a sign of Germany's new power and influence in Europe. Bismarck's prestige as a statesman was also at its height. Yet Germany had been reluctantly pushed into the limelight and was blamed by both sides for their disappointments, as this comment by an Austrian delegate (Baron Schwegel) suggests:

1 Bismarck will certainly have declared to the Russians that he attaches greater importance to the gratification of our wishes than those of England – at the moment he is strikingly, even demonstratively, friendly with Andrassy; but I do not trust him and I am convinced that basically
5 he is only working for the Russians ...
   We discussed the enlargement of Montenegro and the Albanian question. Success was on our side, but the battle was fierce. England, France and Turkey sided with us, and Russia, Germany and Italy were against, i.e. 4 against 3. German friendship seems at times very thread-
10 bare, and I see more and more clearly how honest are the western nations, the English and the French.

Shuvalov, a Russian delegate, summed up his views as follows:

1 You may well ask why we have so far not obtained any better results
backed by the powerful goodwill of Bismarck. It is because we have
been confronted by systematic opposition from England and Austria.
Andrassy, very cordial, acting the gentleman in his talks with me,
5 becomes a different person when in the presence of the English, and
turns into a servile admirer of every word that falls from the lips of
Beaconsfield [Disraeli, the British PM]. The consequence is that
Bismarck, whose chief preoccupation is to avoid clashes, and to bring
the Congress to an end, finds himself forced to tack between the three
10 of them [Britain, Austria and Russia] and does not always exert an energetic goodwill towards us.

The Power most pleased with the Treaty of Berlin was undoubtedly
Britain. Important British interests in the Mediterranean, especially
her naval influence, had been safeguarded and she had acquired
Cyprus as a base to enable her to resist Russian expansion in Asia
Minor. She had even asserted a right to send warships into the Black
Sea whenever she judged it necessary. The Russian influence and
threat to Constantinople had been checked by Britain's preservation
of a good deal of Ottoman power (see the *Punch* cartoon on page 26).
In addition, British co-operation with Austria-Hungary had produced
useful results, so that the unity of the *Dreikaiserbund* had been broken.
It was naturally this last point which caused Bismarck most concern.

4 The Making of the Alliance System, 1879–84

> **KEY ISSUES** Why did Bismarck construct an alliance system? In
> what ways did it increase German security?

1878 marked a turning point in Bismarckian foreign policy. Faced
with Russia's hostility and fearing the creation of an anti-German
coalition, he changed his approach. From now on, he tended to seize
the initiative and attempt to influence events to ensure Germany's
security. This led to the creation of the Bismarckian alliance system –
'an overall political situation in which all the powers except France
have need of us and are . . . kept from forming coalitions against us by
their relations with one another'.

Bismarck's anxieties for Germany's security were much increased
by the Congress of Berlin. The Tsar regarded the Congress as 'a
European coalition against Russia, under the leadership of prince
Bismarck'. Austria-Hungary was co-operating closely with Britain to
enforce the terms of the treaty on the Turks and the Russians. This
left Germany rather on her own and exposed to the full blast of
Russian hostility – spearheaded by the pro-French Pan-Slav faction
around Tsar Alexander II. His displeasure with Bismarck's attitude

"HUMPTY-DUMPTY"!

"HUMPTY-DUMPTY SAT ON A WALL;
HUMPTY-DUMPTY HAD A GREAT FALL:
DIZZY, WITH CYPRUS, AND ALL THE QUEEN'S MEN,
HOPES TO SET HUMPTY-DUMPTY UP AGAIN."

Punch cartoon 'Humpty-Dumpty'.

was made abundantly clear to the Kaiser (whose sympathies were pro-Russian), as this letter of August 1879 suggests:

1 The Turks, sustained by their friends the English and Austrians, who in the meantime firmly hold two Turkish provinces, invaded by them in times of peace ... do not cease to raise difficulties of detail which are of the greatest importance as much for the Bulgars as for the brave Montenegrins ...
5 Decision rests with the majority of the European commissioners. Those of France and Italy join ours on practically all questions, while those of Germany appear to have received the word of command to support the Austrian view which is systematically hostile to us and is so in questions which in no way interest Germany but are very important for us.
10 Forgive, my dear Uncle, the frankness of my language based on the facts, but I think it is my duty to call your attention to the sad consequences which these may cause in our good neighbourly relations by embittering our two nations against each other, as the press of the two countries is already doing.

a) The Dual Alliance, 1879

In 1878–79 it seemed to Bismarck that Germany was presented with a stark choice: either accept the continuing hostility of Russia or form an alliance with her. He was unwilling to choose the latter, since that would alienate Austria-Hungary. The desire for good relations with Russia, he insisted, 'could not extend so far that German policy is permanently subordinated to Russian policy and that we sacrifice our relationship with Austria for Russia's sake'. Hence he put out feelers for an alliance with Austria-Hungary.

The actual proposal he put to Andrassy, the Austrian foreign secretary, in 1879 was a curious one. It envisaged a permanent relationship, creating a sort of 'Germanic bloc' in Europe. As the junior partner in the alliance, Austria-Hungary's Balkan ambitions would be kept in check, while the exclusive tie with Germany would 'dig a ditch' between the Austrians and the western Powers. Yet Andrassy flatly rejected these proposals. Instead, he wanted a defensive pact directed solely against Russia, and this he achieved.

By the terms of the Dual Alliance of October 1879, Germany and Austria promised to give full support if either were attacked by Russia. If the attack came from a Power other than Russia, the ally was only required to observe a benevolent neutrality. The anti-Russian direction of the alliance is thus perfectly clear. The treaty was secret and to last initially for five years, with provision for automatic renewal at three year intervals. This treaty has often been called a landmark because it was not concluded as a prelude to some specific action, like earlier treaties; because it lasted so long; and because, with its precise terms kept secret, it bred suspicion among other Powers, who soon negotiated similar treaties of their own. Eventually Europe was divided into league and counter-league.

b) The Three Emperors' Alliance, 1881

The Austro-German treaty was not ideal from Bismarck's point of view, but it served his purpose well enough. The Russians, getting wind of the negotiations, made known their desire to settle their differences with Germany even before the treaty was signed. Bismarck seized upon this to create a new tripartite alliance, embracing both Russia and Austria-Hungary. More than 18 months elapsed, however, before the new *Dreikaiserbund* was signed in June 1881, indicating that securing agreement to its terms taxed Bismarck's skills to the utmost. The major problem, apart from delays caused by the accession of a new Tsar (Alexander III), was Austria-Hungary's determined opposition to the whole project. Andrassy judged that the Dual Alliance should be the 'tombstone' of the old *Dreikaiserbund*, not a 'stepping stone' towards a new one. In his mind, the alliance with Germany was the first step towards the creation of a powerful anti-Russian bloc, embracing Britain and possibly France. This Austrian resistance persisted throughout 1880, until a change in British policy towards Turkey made them despair of continuing co-operation with her. They therefore yielded to Bismarck's pressure to seek an understanding with Russia over the Balkans.

By the terms of the *Dreikaiserbund* of 1881, each member of the alliance could count on the neutrality of her partners if she was at war with another Power. Germany was thus liberated from the danger of a Franco-Russian combination directed against her. Hence German security was boosted.

The other source of a possible war was the Balkans, and here too the Alliance calmed the situation. It was agreed that the allies would not allow territorial changes in European Turkey without their mutual agreement. Germany, occupying a pivotal role, could expect to moderate the policies of her two allies. They promised to 'take account of their respective interests in the Balkans'. Thus Russia's insistence on the closure of the Straits to warships (especially British) was asserted and the eventual reunion of Bulgaria and Eastern Rumelia was accepted. In return, Russia recognised Austria-Hungary's right to annex Bosnia. The alliance was secret and was to last for three years.

c) The Triple Alliance, 1882

Despite the 1881 *Dreikaiserbund*, a leading Pan-Slav general visited Paris in early 1882, campaigning for a Franco-Russian alliance, and so Bismarck felt uncertain about Russia's reliability. Accordingly the Dual Alliance partners responded favourably in 1882 to Italian approaches for an alliance. Bismarck did not want an alliance with Italy for its own sake. Italy was a second-rate, rather than a Great, Power; and Bismarck was (quite rightly) sceptical of Italy's abilities, remarking privately that she had 'a large appetite but small teeth'. His main object was to increase France's isolation. Against a background of fears of a Franco-Russian alliance, Italy seemed a useful ally against France. Even so, the commitments undertaken were limited.

By the terms of the Triple Alliance of May 1882, both Germany and Italy were entitled to support from each other against an unprovoked attack by France. In the event of an attack by two Powers, all the partners would render mutual assistance. If Austria-Hungary were at war with Russia, Italy would be neutral – thus giving the Austrians security on their southern frontier. In this respect the Triple Alliance served as a useful addition to the Dual Alliance of 1879 with its anti-Russian emphasis, but it did not, as is often said, convert the Dual Alliance of 1879 into the Triple Alliance. The network of alliances was further extended by treaties between Austria-Hungary and Serbia in 1881, and with Rumania in 1883. The following year, the *Dreikaiserbund* was renewed without difficulty for a further three years.

The years 1882 to 1887 marked the zenith of the Bismarckian system, when Bismarck could feel confident that Germany's position in Europe was quite secure. This enabled him to indulge in the luxury of colonial ventures in which he could even seek French co-operation against Britain in Africa.

5 Bismarck and Colonies, 1884–90

> **KEY ISSUE** What were Bismarck's motives in acquiring colonies?

In 1884–85 the absence of serious difficulties with either Russia or France enabled Bismarck to embark on an energetic colonial policy. As a consequence, Germany acquired an overseas empire in various parts of Africa and consolidated her claims to a number of islands in the Pacific. Bismarck's interest in colonies, however, was fairly short-lived. In terms of size, her empire was quite modest by 1890, as well as being economically insignificant.

In the early 1880s, Bismarck had expressed opposition to acquiring colonies, but by 1884 he decided that, after all, they might serve a useful political purpose as well as being of some benefit to the German economy. Industrialists were anxious for new markets for German manufactured goods, and trading companies were complaining of being squeezed out of parts of Africa by foreign rivals.

When Bismarck decided to satisfy these demands for colonies, he assumed that they would be largely self-supporting financially. The government's responsibilities would therefore be limited to granting protection to trading companies, such as the German East Africa Company. Banks and investors would provide the necessary funds to make the colonies economically viable. Yet in these assumptions, Bismarck was to be disappointed. Most of Germany's colonies in

Africa became a financial burden. Furthermore, colonial ventures became a liability in diplomatic affairs. Small wonder that by 1889 he was complaining of being 'sick and tired of colonies'.

In 1884–85 the situation had been quite different. Colonies seemed a good issue to raise in the 1884 elections, as colonialism caught the public mood. Bismarck needed an issue that would weaken the liberal parties in Germany, which had gained strength in the 1881 elections. To bolster his own position as a conservative Chancellor, he also wanted to discredit the groups associated with the Crown Prince who personified the values of English-style liberalism – detested by Bismarck. For such a purpose, a colonial conflict with Britain was ideal – 'a stunt got up for the 1884 elections', as one of Bismarck's advisers later asserted. As such, it served its purpose very well. But he also had diplomatic aims, wishing to improve Franco-German relations by enlisting French support against Britain.

In 1884–85 Bismarck asserted claims to territories in Africa, such as Togo, the Cameroons and South West Africa (see the map on page 45), that challenged existing British commercial or imperial interests. In East Africa he encouraged German traders to establish claims against their British rivals. In collaboration with France, he not only wrecked a conference on Egypt's financial problems but also challenged a rather dubious British manoeuvre to protect her interests in the Congo, insisting that rival claims in the region be submitted to an international conference (see page 47). Bismarck achieved his objectives without difficulty – gaining 1 million square miles of land in total – because the British faced a crisis with Russia over Afghanistan in 1885. Hence, while her diplomatic position was so weak, she could not afford to antagonise Germany in colonial matters.

Only a year later, however, the diplomatic tide had turned in Britain's favour. The Franco-German colonial *entente* had been replaced by a renewal of tension. More serious still, Russo-German relations were badly strained after a new crisis in the Balkans. By 1890, when a second partition agreement was being negotiated over East Africa, the roles were reversed compared with 1886. An official observed that 'a good understanding with England means much more to Bismarck than the whole of East Africa'. As a result, Germany made substantial concessions to Britain in this area.

Most historians agree that though Bismarck may have used imperialism as a way of distracting attention from social problems in Germany (hence the phrase 'social imperialism'), his interest in colonial matters was short-lived and that his policy was subordinate to his assessment of the international situation. Thus, in 1884–85, when European affairs were favourable to Germany, he played the colonial game with great vigour. Yet he seems to have become disillusioned with it remarkably quickly, and by 1888 he was resisting demands for further colonial expansion on the grounds of Germany's continental security. In a classic phrase he asserted: 'My map of Africa lies in Europe. Here is Russia and here is France, and we are in the middle'.

6 The Bismarckian System under Pressure, 1885–90

> **KEY ISSUE** How assured was peace between the Great Powers in this period?

a) Renewed Bulgarian Problems

In 1885 a revolt broke out in Eastern Rumelia, in favour of union with Bulgaria. This demand contravened the Treaty of Berlin which, at Britain's insistence, had deliberately divided the two provinces. Britain, assuming that Russia would dominate Bulgaria, had wished the Bulgarian state to be as small as possible. The Russians, however, had created widespread resentment in Bulgaria in the early 1880s by treating it as their satellite. As a result, the Bulgarians expelled all Russian officials. When, on top of this insult, the Prince of Bulgaria accepted the demands of the Rumelian movement for unity, the Tsar's indignation knew no bounds.

At a meeting of representatives of the Great Powers, the Russians naturally condemned the revolt as a violation of the Berlin Treaty. Germany and Austria-Hungary supported their fellow member of the Three Emperors' Alliance. But the British took a different line. Now that the Bulgars had thrown off Russian control, Britain suggested that the two provinces be linked by a 'Personal Union' under the Prince of Bulgaria. An enlarged independent Bulgaria was expected to be better able to check Russian influence in the Balkans. This British proposal was eventually adopted when France and Italy decided to back it.

The Tsar got his revenge by forcing the Prince of Bulgaria to abdicate, and it seemed possible that Russian forces would invade. This was too much for Austria-Hungary. In November 1886, she warned the Russians against further interference in Bulgaria even though Germany would not support her. How would Bismarck react?

Bismarck made clear his refusal to take sides in this dispute in a statement to the Reichstag in early 1887: 'It is a matter of complete indifference to Germany who rules in Bulgaria and what becomes of her'. This statement of neutrality did not satisfy the Tsar, however, who refused to renew the *Dreikaiserbund,* which now ended. Bismarck feared that unless he made a positive gesture towards Russia, the Tsar might yield to Pan-Slavist pressure for an alliance with France. He therefore decided on a bold step – proposing a secret Russo-German alliance.

b) The Reinsurance Treaty, 1887

By the terms of this treaty, Germany recognised Russia's right to a preponderant influence in Bulgaria. She also agreed to Russian control of the Straits if her security required it. If either Power was at war, the other would remain neutral – unless France or Austria-Hungary were the object of attack. This proviso was highly significant. The Russians had demanded a free hand to attack Austria-Hungary, but Bismarck refused to give it to them. In return, Germany forfeited the free hand to attack France which she had enjoyed under the 1881 alliance. Bismarck seemingly put such a high premium on Russia's friendship in 1887 that he was prepared to contravene the spirit, if not the letter, of the Austro-German alliance of 1879. That alliance, after all, had been directed specifically against Russia. Furthermore, as an entice-ment to Russia, he let it be known, unofficially, that he had 'absolutely nothing against Russia going as far as Constantinople and taking the Dardanelles'. He was undoubtedly playing a dangerous game. Although wishing to prevent war, he might in fact be hastening one by encouraging Russian ambitions.

Bismarck's fears for Germany's security had grown considerably in late 1886 and early 1887. Russia and Austria-Hungary appeared to be on the brink of war over the Balkans. In addition, there was a spirit of revenge (*revanchism*) emerging again in France, associated with the popular and politically ambitious figure of General Boulanger. To add to Bismarck's difficulties, the Italians were demanding greater recognition for their interests in the Mediterranean as the price of renewing the Triple Alliance, due to expire in May 1887. This prob-lem was settled relatively easily. Germany and Austria-Hungary prom-ised support for Italian interests in North Africa and the Balkans. When, in addition, the British government made a loose agreement with Italy and Austria-Hungary to defend the existing state of affairs (*status quo*) in the Mediterranean, a solution to the main problem facing Bismarck began to emerge.

c) The Mediterranean Agreements, 1887

Bismarck realised that he had to persuade Britain to play a more important role in European affairs. Certainly if Britain would do more to resist Russia in the Near East, this would have beneficial effects. Russia might well be restrained from adopting too aggressive a stance over Bulgaria, and furthermore Austria-Hungary might find in London the sympathetic response to her desire for support which would calm her fears. Bismarck therefore exerted all his influence to encourage Britain to conclude a formal agreement with Italy and Austria-Hungary to defend the *status quo* in both the Mediterranean and the Near East.

The Second Mediterranean Agreement, signed in December 1887, was not a formal alliance, but it did signal Britain's willingness to check Russia in Bulgaria and at the Straits. If necessary, Austrian troops and British warships, with Italian backing, would be deployed. This combination deterred the Russians from resorting to force. As an inducement for the Russians to sign the Reinsurance Treaty, Bismarck had dangled before their eyes the enticing possibility of their control of the Dardanelles. Now Britain had pulled his chestnuts out of the fire.

d) Russo-German Relations

Despite the Reinsurance Treaty, Russo-German relations never regained their former cordiality. Bismarck was partly to blame for this. At the end of 1887, Russia was denied access to the Berlin money market for loans to finance her industrialisation. As a result, Russia turned to Paris for loans, foreshadowing the alliance between France and Russia which took place, in 1894, after Bismarck's fall.

Even before Bismarck fell from office in 1890, some were questioning the basic assumptions of his foreign policy, especially his wish to keep on good terms with Russia. The anti-Russian sentiments of Wilhelm II, who became Kaiser in 1888, were shared by many influential people in Germany. Both industrial and agrarian groups regarded Russia's economic modernisation as a threat to their interests. In military circles there was serious talk of the need for a preventive war against Russia before she became too powerful. Perhaps even Bismarck had had his doubts. Was this why he proposed an alliance with Britain in 1889? The Kaiser, however, accepted the case made by his advisers against the renewal of the Reinsurance Treaty. Disagreement between him and Bismarck over the Russian alliance was one of the issues which led to Bismarck's resignation in 1890.

7 Bismarck's Foreign Policy, 1871–90: Success or Failure?

> **KEY ISSUE** What conclusions can we reach about Bismarck's foreign policy?

A statesman's success or failure is not something that can usually be measured with great precision, but historians have devised a number of yardsticks that can be helpful. The most obvious of these is how far a statesman achieves his aims. The complexities of the problems facing a leader are also relevant to an assessment of his achievements. In particular, the amount of choice – the options open – should be taken into account. Another consideration is whether the policies pursued produced solutions that were lasting or only brought short-term advantages.

In the case of Bismarck's foreign policy, the aims are quite clear, as are the problems Germany faced. He made decisions from a limited number of options available to him.

In the short term, Bismarck's success was very great. He wished to prevent war, and under his leadership Germany enjoyed security and Europe was blessed with peace for 20 years. In this time Germany was able to become the strongest industrial power on the continent. He prevented an anti-German coalition, especially by keeping France isolated, and he helped prevent Austria and Russia from coming to blows in the Balkans. His alliance system had to be constantly repaired, but it was still standing in 1890, when Bismarck fell from power.

To his admirers, Bismarck was 'the Napoleon of alliances', just as Berlin was the diplomatic capital of Europe. They draw a sharp contrast between his successes, and in general his shrewd and realistic understanding of foreign relations, and the abysmal failures of his successors, who ended up in 1914 with a major war which Germany lost. Bismarck knew where to stop: he did not attempt to construct a fleet that would challenge Britain and he did not attempt to expand in Europe beyond Germany's 1871 borders.

To critics, however, Bismarck was not a great statesman. He was indeed a cause of friction, encouraging mutual suspicions between rivals, for instance between France and Britain in Africa. Here was a man who wanted to maintain tension in Europe so that, as an arbiter, he could gain prestige at home. In addition, his alliance system, by its secret diplomacy, bred suspicion and insecurity. Furthermore, his system was breaking down by the late 1880s, as France and Russia moved closer together. In some ways the First World War was his legacy.

Some writers believe that Bismarck chose the wrong option in 1881. With the Three Emperor's Alliance, he brought two potential enemies (Austria and Russia) into an alignment that was unnatural and was doomed to failure – because the causes of antagonism between them still existed. What was the point of trying to 'square the circle' of Austro-Russian enmity? Instead, perhaps he should have reinforced the Austro-German alliance by seeking British support against Russia. Admittedly, this might have created a Franco-Russian partnership, which he called the 'nightmare of coalitions'. But was the force of *revanchism* in France, or of Pan-Slavism in Russia, really as great as he feared? Why did he not take more account of Alexander III's aversion to the republican regime in France? Admittedly France and Russia formed an alliance in the 1890s and fought as allies from 1914, but we should not imagine that their solidarity was inevitable. Perhaps he should have directed his considerable energy and skill towards effecting a reconciliation with France. Or would such an effort have been unrealistic and doomed to failure?

By the late 1880s, Bismarck seems to have become pessimistic, even fatalistic. He remarked to a general, 'The task of our policy is, if possible, to prevent war and if that is not possible at least to postpone it'. Contemporary opinion in Germany found this policy stultifying – a 'healthy war was preferable to a morbid peace', it was said. A German diplomat commented in early 1888: 'Here, everyone is for war, with almost the sole exception of Bismarck'. Others demanded the abandonment of Bismarck's European-centred diplomacy for a policy of overseas expansion. His most influential critics insisted that the Reinsurance Treaty, due to expire in 1890, was both contradictory and dangerous. After Bismarck's resignation in 1890, the alliance with Russia was not renewed.

In 1890 Bismarck was replaced. His critics took over. Ironically, it was they who would use the power Bismarck had bequeathed to them. It was they who would help to decide the long-term significance of his work.

Working on Chapter 2

As you read this chapter, give close attention to three aspects: 1) The use of alliances to counter threats to Germany's security; 2) The Eastern Question; and 3) An assessment of Bismarck. You will be well advised to study the maps carefully. You may also need to reread your notes from Chapter 1, on the key features of the Eastern Question. Because there are so many events covered for this chapter, it might be useful to draw up a comprehensive time-chart to show what happened and in what order.

Answering structured and essay questions on Chapter 2

The tools needed to answer both AS and A2 questions are, first, common sense and, second, knowledge. Common sense is needed to understand exactly what a question requires you to do and also to decide which aspects of your knowledge to deploy to answer it. So always read a question carefully, mull it over in your mind, establish its parameters, perhaps break it down into smaller, more manageable questions, and make sure that you perform the task that it requires of you – not a task you'd prefer to do. You must answer the question, the whole question and nothing but the question. The factual knowledge you need should be relatively easily acquired by working through this chapter carefully and thoroughly.

A wide variety of questions can be set, but most will focus on one of three issues: the influence of Balkan problems on Bismarck's diplomacy; the Congress of Berlin's solutions to the Eastern Question; and the success/failure of Bismarck's foreign policy

Most structured questions contain several parts which require mainly factual answers and a more analytical final part which builds upon the earlier ones and requires more analysis. Consider the following:

Summary Diagram
Bismarck and Europe, 1871–90

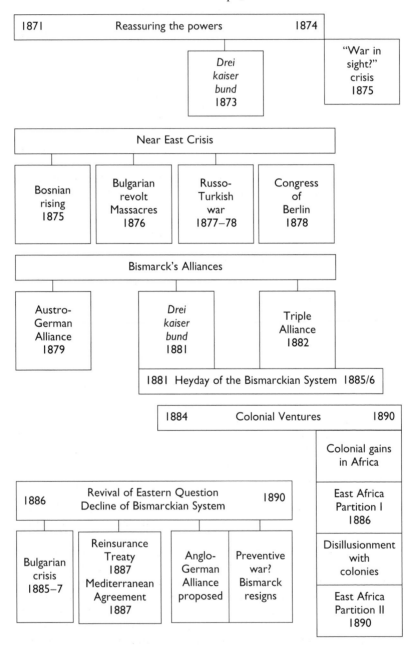

a) Why were relations between France and Germany so poor after 1871? (5 marks)
b) What measures did Bismarck take to isolate France after 1871? (15 marks)
c) How successful was Bismarck's policy towards France between 1871 and 1890? (30 marks)

Answering this structured question should be relatively straightforward – but do be aware of the mark-scheme and budget your time accordingly. Part a) is worth least marks, so do not spend too much time on it. Clearly you will mention the terms of the Treaty of Frankfurt, and especially the loss of Alsace and Lorraine. What other causes of friction were there? Part b) demands knowledge of Bismarck's alliances. Part c) requires more thought. Clearly you will draw on many of the points you made in the earlier two parts. Did Bismarck's alliances solve the friction? Clearly not. But did they contain it in the relevant period? You must here engage with the vexed issue of whether Bismarck's 'system' was breaking down by 1890. You will need to make some reference to better Franco-Russian relations.

Consider also the following essay questions

1. 'His concern was the security of the German Empire; his achievement was the domination of Europe.' Discuss this view of Bismarck's foreign policy.
2. Was Bismarck's foreign policy 1871–90 a success?
3. 'At the Congress of Berlin in 1878 the complicated Eastern Question was successfully dealt with by negotiation'. Discuss this statement.
4. Why did the Eastern Question threaten European peace in the years 1875–78? How far did the Treaty of Berlin provide a satisfactory solution?

Remember the importance of defining the terms used in a question. What is meant in Question 1, for instance, by 'security' and 'domination'? Even more important is an understanding of the possible meanings of 'success' in Question 2. For 3 and 4 the 'Eastern Question' will need to be defined. Remember also the importance of dividing up these, perhaps forbiddingly, large questions into smaller ones. Your work on structured questions should here pay off. Imagine that the essay questions above are the final parts of a structured question. What might the earlier parts be? For instance, for Question 2 you could have separate questions on particular aspects of Bismarck's foreign policy, how successful he was a) at isolating France, b) at minimising friction between Russia and Austria-Hungary, and so on. The most daunting question becomes much simpler if broken down into convenient component parts. For Question 3, you might consider the successes and then the failures of the Congress of Berlin, before coming to a balanced verdict. Question 4 is already in two parts. How might each part be divided?

Source-based questions on Chapter 2

1 The Congress of Berlin, 1878

Read carefully the extracts from the writings of Austrian and Russian diplomats at the Congress of Berlin, given on pages 24–5, and study the cartoon from *Punch* on page 26. Answer the following questions:

a) Who are **i)** Andrassy, and **ii)** Beaconsfield? (2 marks)

b) Which country, Austria or Russia, seems to be more displeased with Bismarck? What does this displeasure suggest about the expectations of that country? (8 marks)

c) Which extract comes closer to identifying Bismarck's motives at the Congress? Explain your answer. (15 marks)

d) Which three 'countries' do the characters in the cartoon represent? (3 marks)

e) What does the artist wish you to believe about the part Disraeli played at the Congress of Berlin? Explain your answer. (8 marks)

f) What is the artist's attitude towards **i)** Turkey, and, **ii)** Cyprus? Support your answers with evidence. (4 marks)

g) Using these sources and your own knowledge, estimate how far the various participants at the Congress of Berlin were satisfied by its decisions. (25 marks)

3 Colonial Rivalries, 1870–1914

POINTS TO CONSIDER

This period saw a remarkable upsurge of imperial activity, including the partition of Africa, the pegging out of 'spheres of influence' in China, and tension – and indeed war – between the major Powers. In short, it is a remarkably important but also remarkably complex period. As you read the chapter, focus first on what happened. A knowledge of the sequence of events will enable you to judge how adequate the theories which seek to explain what happened really are. Pay particular attention to the effects of imperial expansion on the relations between the major Powers. In this way, you will see that this chapter is an integral part of the whole book, rather than a 'dispensable' section.

KEY DATES

1857	Indian Mutiny.
1869	Suez Canal opens.
1877	King Leopold sets up the International Association.
1881–2	French protectorate proclaimed over Tunisia.
1882	British forces invade Egypt, defeating Arabi Pasha.
1884–5	The Berlin Conference.
1885	British protectorate proclaimed over the Niger region.
1886	Gold discovered in the Transvaal.
1889	British South Africa Company receives a Royal Charter.
1890	Heligoland-Zanzibar Treaty.
1895	Japanese victory in the war with China.
1896	Italians defeated at Adowa.
1898	Battle of Omdurman; Fashoda incident.
1899–1902	Boer War.
1900	Boxer Rebellion in China.
1902	Anglo-Japanese alliance.
1905	Japanese victory in the war with Russia.

1 The Great Powers and Colonies before 1870

KEY ISSUE Was the mid-19th century a period of anti-imperialism?

European expansion overseas began long before industrialisation. The great 'Age of Discovery' was the sixteenth century, not the nineteenth. Between 1450 and 1815 Spain and Portugal, followed by Holland, France and Britain, acquired overseas empires in Africa, the Americas, India and South East Asia. Some were colonies of white settlement, such as North America; some were plantation colonies, in which a European élite employed slave labour, such as the West Indian sugar islands; while others were little more than trading bases.

In the early nineteenth century Britain, as the Duke of Wellington observed, 'had possession of nearly every valuable port and colony in the world'. Serious doubts existed, however, whether overseas possessions (India excepted) were, in Disraeli's phrase, anything but 'millstones around our neck'. Indeed in 1865 a Parliamentary Report recommended that Britain should abandon her few possessions in West Africa. The period 1815 to 1870 has therefore been seen by some writers as an age of 'anti-imperialism'.

There was undoubtedly some disillusionment with colonies in mid-nineteenth-century Britain. Colonial settlers were widely thought to be ungrateful towards the 'Mother Country' and too quick to demand independence. The American colonists, for example, had thrown off their allegiance to Britain after 1776, and the Canadians, among others, contributed little – and that reluctantly – to the costs of their own defence. An observer commented in 1865, 'The normal course of colonial history is the perpetual assertion of the right to self-government'. In response to such demands, Britain did grant more control over their own affairs to settlers in such colonies as Canada and Cape Colony (South Africa).

Furthermore, by about 1850 the economic justification for colonies was wearing thin. The practice of regulating the trade of the colonies to suit the interests of the Mother Country (known as the 'old colonial system') ceased to seem worthwhile. It was noted that Britain did more trade with America after independence than before it. The colonies were no longer Britain's best trading partners, and the regulations of the 'old colonial system' were replaced by free trade. Britain's economic supremacy over her European rivals had little to do with empire.

Yet despite this so-called mood, Britain did not actually give up an existing colony of any significance in the period 1815–1870. Rather the reverse, in fact. Singapore, Aden, Hong Kong and Lagos became British possessions, acquired, in the main, as trading stations or naval bases. Australia and New Zealand also became colonies, following a revival of interest in emigration to absorb over-population at home. Furthermore, British rule in India was extended. India was 'the jewel of the crown'; and, apart from considerations of power and prestige, Britain's trade with India was important and seemed to require a British political presence. In addition, the cost of defending India, unlike Canada and elsewhere, was borne from local revenues. After the Indian Mutiny of 1857, therefore, the British government took over administration from the East India Company. Equally important, as well as extending her 'formal empire', Britain extended her influence – which could amount to 'informal empire' – in other areas of the world, including Latin America. That this was a period of 'anti-imperialism' in Britain therefore cannot be accepted.

This mid-nineteenth century period also saw both France and Russia extending their empires. French imperialism was mainly a quest for prestige, although it was sometimes encouraged by interest groups such as the Lyons silk industry. Algeria became a colony of settlement in the two decades following the initial conquest in 1830. In the previous decade French power in Senegal, in West Africa, was extended under a remarkably dynamic colonial governor. His creation of well-trained African regiments, the Senegalese *tirailleurs* (sharpshooters), laid the base for French military imperialism in West Africa. In the 1860s French control was also being asserted over parts of Indo-China.

The military also played a key role in the Russian land-based imperialism that alarmed the Government of India because it brought Russian forces to within striking distance of Afghanistan, adjacent to India's north west frontier. The Russian advance began in the 1840s and continued at a faster tempo in the 1860s. The capture of Tashkent and Bokhara put most of Turkestan under Russian control. Further east, Russia secured the territory that made the Tsarist Empire a neighbour of China, obtaining in addition an outlet on the Pacific Ocean, the future Vladivostok. Once begun, the conquest of turbulent peoples on Russia's borders could be almost infinitely extended on the grounds that the really secure frontier always lay further ahead.

Hence in a supposedly 'anti-imperialist' age, three of the European Powers extended their political or economic influence over non-European states or societies. The reasons for this were varied. In some cases it was to assist trade; in others prestige was the main consideration. Frequently, especially where existing frontiers were being pushed forward, the impetus for expansion came from 'the men on the spot', rather than from political leaders in the capitals of Europe. A similar mixture of motives continued to influence European imperialism in the later decades of the century.

2 Africa and the Europeans before 1870

> **KEY ISSUE** In what ways did the Victorians stereotype Africa?

a) The Victorian Misunderstanding of Africa

To most Victorians, Africa was the 'Dark Continent'. They assumed that the continent had no history and that the Africans themselves were virtually unchanged since prehistoric times. From this false assumption it was but a short step to an imaginary 'Darkest Africa' sunk in barbarism. Thus the absence of divisions into European-style states or nations was interpreted as a sign that anarchy reigned. The diversity of the peoples of Africa was often neglected in favour of stereotypes. Instead of there being millions of Africans, all individuals and all different, they spoke of 'the African'; and the apparent savagery of some tribes or the laziness of others, which were largely the product of sensationalist explorers' tales, were regarded as typical. 'Darkest Africa' was seemingly inhabited by culturally and racially inferior peoples, devoted to superstitious pagan rites. At best they were children, at worst savages. In either case they needed a firm hand from superior white Europeans, as well as the Bible to teach them the benefits of civilisation and Christianity.

Whites towards the end of the nineteenth century believed that there was a hierarchy among races, just as there was among species in the animal kingdom. The lighter the skin, so ran their simplistic message, the higher the race on the evolutionary scale. Most nineteenth-century Europeans naively regarded racism as a science, in which the size of the skull or the angle at which the jaw jutted forward were seen as unmistakable signs of African inferiority.

b) Political Changes

In political terms, a number of significant developments took place between 1815 and 1870. In North Africa, French rule was firmly established in Algeria. European influence was also growing in Tunisia and Egypt, and to some extent in Tripoli. These three states were still under the nominal control of the Sultan of Turkey. In South Africa, European rule was steadily expanding despite local resistance. The Boers, descendants of the original Dutch settlers, established new settlements outside British control. The Transvaal and Orange Free State were recognised by Britain as independent republics in the 1850s. Although the British government attempted fitfully to protect the interests of black Africans, its main concern was the Cape. Cape Colony was regarded as a vital base on the route to India – both before and after the opening of the Suez Canal in 1869. In 1872 Cape Colony was granted self-government, but this did not mean the end of the British government's involvement in the affairs of South Africa.

In sub-Saharan Africa (i.e. south of the Sahara desert), major changes were taking place in tribal power relationships. This is an aspect of what some writers call 'the African partition of Africa'. The term covers a series of complex events such as the *jihads* (holy wars) of the Islamic empires in the northerly parts of West Africa and the *mfecane* (the Zulu despotism) in southern Africa. The friendly response of some African tribes to the European presence later in the century was sometimes the result of their experiences in these internal wars. To the defeated and displaced tribes, Europeans might well seem lesser evils or even potential allies.

c) Economic Change

The economic penetration of Africa by Europe was also well under way, especially in North Africa, whose states were much more closely integrated into the economy of Europe than was most of sub-Saharan Africa. The size of the European commercial communities in these states was growing. European goods such as cotton cloth, firearms and spirits, as well as Indian and American textiles, were found in many parts of Africa before 1870. The major economic change taking place was the gradual decline of the slave trade. Although many European states had agreed in 1815 to follow Britain's lead in abolishing the slave trade, in practice there was much evasion for several decades. However, in West Africa, where the ban on slaving was enforced by the British navy, a thriving trade in tropical products developed. In addition to palm oil (in demand as a machine lubricant and for soap), vegetable oils, timber, ivory and gum were in great demand in Europe.

From Sierra Leone to the Niger, Britain enjoyed a sort of 'informal empire' on the cheap. Four naval stations and a few consuls were enough for the exercise of British political and economic influence. But, apart from trading stations, territorial acquisitions were generally neither wanted nor necessary at this time.

In West-Central Africa (the Congo and Angola), where British naval patrols were few, the slave trade actually expanded for some decades, becoming so profitable that slavers penetrated up to a thousand miles inland. The sudden cessation of the trade in the 1850s, when Portugal at last prohibited the trade to Brazil, disrupted the economy of the region.

East Africa's commercial links were with Arabia and India, not Europe. The island of Zanzibar became the centre of a thriving trade in ivory, gum and cloves as well as slaves, despite British attempts to persuade the Sultan of Zanzibar to abolish the slave trade. Some European merchants were also attempting to create trading ventures in the region.

In the course of the period 1815 to 1870, therefore, the commercial links between Europe and most regions of Africa were growing stronger with each decade. Africa's trade expanded and she became more closely integrated into the international economy. In other respects, however, the gap between Africa and Europe was widening. World trade was expanding at a much faster rate than the African economy as a whole. Nor was it, of course, just a question of disparity in *economic growth*. Despite the vitality of African life, the encounter between Africans and Europeans after 1870 did not take place on equal terms. The rapid technological advance of the leading European states – in the form of steamships and railways and the deadly weapons of war – meant that an imbalance of *power* existed between Europeans and Africans by about 1870.

d) Historical Interpretations

As knowledge of Africa's rich past has increased, so many earlier assumptions about the nature of African societies have needed to be reconsidered. Historians no longer accept the prejudiced Victorian views of their impact on Africa. Thus the traditional view that the Europeans 'shaped a passive Africa to their will' is not tenable. Vitality, rather than passivity, seems more appropriate to describe Africa in 1870. Imperialism should therefore be regarded as a process of interaction, in which Europeans and Africans were reacting to changes that were taking place both in Europe and Africa.

3 Colonial Rivalry and the Scramble for Africa

> **KEY ISSUES** What were the key events in the partition of the continent? To what extent were Great Power rivalries involved?

The partition of Africa amongst the Great Powers was accomplished in about 20 years, roughly 1880–1900. As striking as the speed was the sheer scale of what happened. In 1880 only one-tenth of Africa had been under *European* rule; by 1900 only about one-tenth was now under *African* rule (see the map on page 45). To the existing colonial rulers of Britain, France, Spain and Portugal were now added Germany, Italy and Belgium. From a European perspective, the partition of Africa resembled a headlong rush to acquire colonial possessions.

In effect, there were two stages to the partition. Firstly, the Powers staked out claims to territory and lines were drawn on a map of Africa, usually in total disregard of the realities of tribal relationships. This stage often amounted to little more than a 'paper partition'. Then, during the 1890s, the serious business of conquest and consolidation began. Even then, most colonial governments were weak, and in both conquest and consolidation Europeans were often dependent on the co-operation and assistance of friendly tribes. African chiefs were persuaded to sign treaties with European officials or commercial agents which, initially, granted some rather vague jurisdiction or influence. This was empire 'on the cheap', and indicates how reluctant governments were to take on the expense of creating proper colonial administrations.

As the Scramble began, the Powers asserted claims to political influence or territorial control in Egypt, West Africa, the Congo, southern Africa and East Africa. Britain was at the centre of affairs, and at one time or another was involved in rivalry with virtually every other European Power. There was indeed an anti-British element to the Scramble for Africa. This is not surprising since Britain had used her sea-power to assert a sort of 'paramountcy' over most of Africa's

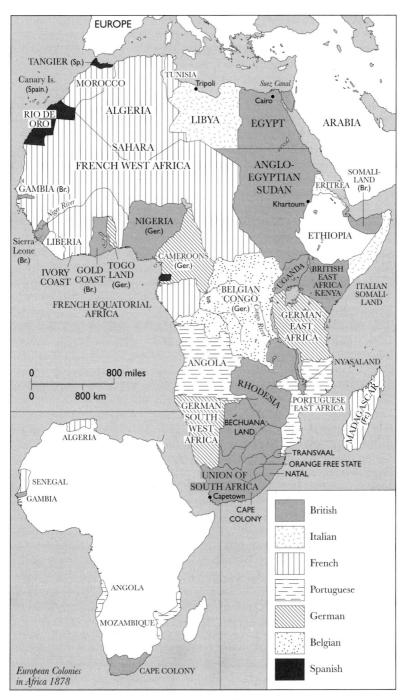

The partition of Africa: 1878 and 1914.

coast in the mid-nineteenth century. One of the few rivalries in which Britain was not directly involved was the assertion of a French protectorate over Tunisia in 1881–82, which angered the Italians, whose nationals greatly outnumbered French residents in the area. Egyptian nationalists were also alarmed by France's action, fearing a similar fate would befall their country.

a) Egypt and After

A joint Franco-British supervision of Egypt's finances had been set up following a declaration of bankruptcy in 1878. When the ruler, the Khedive, was deposed for intriguing against the Dual Control of France and Britain, resentment against foreign interference rapidly increased. A nationalist movement, led by an army officer, Arabi Pasha, seemed to threaten the Dual Control. In Britain, the 'anti-imperialist' Liberal government under Gladstone hesitated and was partly pushed and partly drifted into a confrontation with Arabi Pasha. Anti-foreign riots and the British bombardment of Alexandria in July 1882 escalated the crisis so that the safety of the Suez Canal (which shortened the route to India and in which Britain had acquired a controlling interest in 1875) was thought to be at risk. The British government, deserted by France at a critical moment, despatched an expeditionary force which defeated Arabi Pasha's army in September 1882. Gladstone insisted that he had not 'invaded' Egypt: Britain had merely 'intervened' and would withdraw 'as soon as possible'. But given the political chaos then existing, Britain remained to restore stability. She was there for 40 years!

Egypt became a contentious issue with France. It was a Frenchman, de Lesseps, who had built the Suez Canal in the 1860s, and French sensitivities would only have been satisfied by a British withdrawal; but this was made less likely by a revolt in the Sudan, which Egypt controlled. The Egyptian army was defeated by the rebel forces, while the cost of the military operations destroyed Egypt's precarious finances, which now needed an international loan to restore solvency. Supervision of the country's financial administration was subsequently placed in the hands of an international commission, on which the French and Russian delegates opposed British proposals. Consequently, in order to be able to govern Egypt, Britain needed German support on the debt commission. Thus, until the financial position of the Egyptian government became much stronger, Bismarck was able to purse a policy of benign blackmail – the 'Egyptian lever'. The price for Germany's support was colonial concessions in Africa and elsewhere. The Scramble had definitely begun.

b) West Africa

In West Africa, French activity greatly increased in the late 1870s and early 1880s. This provoked Britain into asserting a formal 'protectorate' over areas where she had previously exerted only an informal influence. A good example of this is the Niger delta, where British companies had been trading for decades. The intrusion of two French trading companies in the 1880s and the appearance of French warships along the coast signalled the intensification of Anglo-French rivalry. In response, Britain made treaties with local chiefs which enabled the British government to declare a formal protectorate over the Niger region in 1885.

Another development which contributed to the scramble was the revival of ambitious schemes for French expansion into what was called the Western Soudan. This was to be achieved through the creation of a railway network that would link Senegal, Algeria and the Upper Niger. The railways, it was believed, would develop a trade estimated at 100 million francs a year. The reality was different: after 20 years, the export trade of this new 'Eldorado' amounted to a mere 3 million francs a year. The railway scheme was mostly abandoned but it nevertheless gave the green light to the French imperialist groups in Senegal. The eventual creation of a vast French empire in West Africa in the 1880s and 1890s was largely the achievement of the French colonial army, frequently acting contrary to instructions from Paris.

c) Berlin Conference

Important as were the Niger and the Nile in terms of Anglo-French rivalry, it was the Congo that fully highlighted the competitiveness of the so-called 'New Imperialism' of the 1880s.

Leopold, King of the Belgians, intended to exploit the economic potential of the Congo (ivory and rubber) for personal financial gain. He set up an International Association in 1877 to open up the region, and this attracted widespread support in Europe. Thus began one of the most remarkable 'confidence tricks' of the age – the projection of a profit-making scheme as a scientific and humanitarian endeavour. The International Association actively concluded treaties with African chiefs in the Congo and, though they were clearly commercial in nature, they were later claimed to have transferred sovereignty over the region to the Association. This provoked France into making rival claims.

The British government tried to counter French claims by concluding a treaty with Portugal, recognising her ancient, if shadowy, claims to the area. France and Germany, however, objected to this 'private arrangement'. Consequently the question was submitted to an international conference, which took place at Berlin from November 1884 to February 1885.

The Berlin Conference gave formal recognition to European claims to territory in Africa and laid down the 'ground rules' for the partition over the next few years. The Congo Free State was recognised as a sovereign state with guarantees of freedom of commerce to all nations. The doctrine of 'effective occupation' laid down at the conference was intended to put a stop to Britain's practice of asserting a vague right to 'influence' over many parts of Africa. It thereby obliged the Powers to define their claims with some precision and reinforce them with tangible signs of their presence. At the Berlin Conference, Germany also formalised her claims to Togo and the Cameroons, German East Africa and South West Africa.

d) Anglo-German Rivalry

German involvement in African affairs was a new factor in the 1880s and an important aspect of the 'New Imperialism'. Colonial issues offered a unique opportunity for Franco-German co-operation – directed against Britain. Bismarck's proposal in 1884 for a Franco-German front struck a responsive chord with Jules Ferry, the French premier and an ardent colonialist. Revenge for her exclusion from Egypt could be combined with the assertion of French claims in west Africa and the Congo. Bismarck also had a grievance against Britain in South West Africa which led him to retaliate against what he regarded as British arrogance towards German interests there. Angered by the endless delays in his negotiations with Britain, Bismarck decided in August 1884 to defend the interests of a German trading company by asserting a claim to South West Africa. The significance of this move was that southern Africa, hitherto an almost exclusively British preserve, became involved in Great Power rivalries.

In 1886 the economic and political situation in southern Africa was revolutionised by the discovery of gold in the Transvaal. From being a poor pastoral farming community, the Transvaal became potentially the wealthiest state in southern Africa and a threat to British imperial interests. This was because the growing economic power of the Transvaal not only put the dominance of Cape Colony at risk, but also threatened to weaken the loyalty of the Cape Boers to British rule. How then were imperial interests in southern Africa to be defended?

One answer was to establish a British presence in Rhodesia (today's Zimbabwe) to act as a counterweight to the Boer republic of the Transvaal. This was the solution offered by Cecil Rhodes. Rhodes, an Englishman who had made a fortune out of diamond mining, was an influential figure in Cape politics. In October 1889, he persuaded the British government to grant a royal charter to his British South Africa Company to administer Rhodesia. In this way the threat to imperial interests was checked – and at no cost to the Treasury. Under Rhodes' guidance, Rhodesia would strengthen the British element in southern Africa.

Britain and Germany were also rivals in East Africa in the 1880s. To further German interests in the territories of the Sultan of Zanzibar, Bismarck exploited the 'Egyptian lever'. A German protectorate was proclaimed over German East Africa (later Tanganyika) in 1885. British commercial interests now redoubled their efforts to secure government backing. This resulted in a partition agreement in 1886, which recognised Germany's stronger claims. Continuing rivalry, involving the risk of serious clashes between British and German groups, made a further partition treaty necessary in 1890. This second agreement, known as the Heligoland-Zanzibar Treaty, was much to Britain's advantage and included a protectorate over the dominions of the Sultan of Zanzibar.

WOOING THE AFRICAN VENUS.
(Some way after Homer's Hymn to Aphrodite.)

[A Charter has just been granted to the Imperial British East Africa Company. This Company will now administer and develop a territory with an estimated area of about 50,000 square miles, including some of the most fertile and salubrious regions of Eastern Africa.]

THE force, O Muse, and functions now unfold | From all earth's nations, Frenchman, Por- | Whose minds are mainly set upon that love:
Of Afric's Venus, graced with mines of gold; | tuguese, [seas, | The Briton, proud as Ægis-bearing Jove,
Who e'en in BISMARCK lights love's furious | From Yankee shores and from all Europe's | Who deems her indeviriginate, her eyes
fire, | Adventurous patriots crowd to seek and share | Being black and burning, like her own fierce
And makes all men woo her with hot desire. | Love of the Libyan Venus. Three there are | skies.

e) Anglo-French Rivalry

The 1890s saw a new intensity to Anglo-French rivalries, especially in West Africa and the Nile valley. In addition Italy was also making a bid for territory in East Africa, especially in the area known as the Horn, including Ethiopia and Eritrea. By 1896, however, the Italians were in serious difficulties. When they were defeated by the Ethiopians at the battle of Adowa, their hopes of creating a large Italian empire in East Africa were dashed.

European diplomatic considerations now came into play. The German government feared for the survival of the Italian monarchy and regime if it suffered a further setback, and therefore Britain was pressed to intervene. In 1896 a force under General Kitchener was sent from Egypt to the Sudan, to take the pressure off the Italian forces threatened by the local force of Dervishes. In 1898 Kitchener advanced southwards and, having defeated the Dervishes in a great battle at Omdurman (with the loss of 48 of his men, compared with 12,000 of the opposition), re-occupied Khartoum. By this time a small French force under Captain Marchand had finally reached Fashoda, on the Upper Nile, 400 miles further south. The aim of Marchand's expedition was to reinforce France's demand for an international conference on Egypt and the Sudan which, they believed, would require Britain to evacuate Egypt. This was a dangerous game for France to play.

The British government responded by demanding the unconditional withdrawal of Marchand's men. Paris was sensitive to clamour to defend France's honour, but the British cabinet vetoed concessions (see the cartoon from *Punch* on page 51). It was this refusal to compromise that made the confrontation at Fashoda a possible prelude to war between the two countries. The French government, however, conscious of Britain's overwhelming naval superiority, eventually climbed down. In November 1898 Marchand was ordered to withdraw from Fashoda.

f) Southern Africa and After

Southern Africa also presented a problem for the British government in the 1890s. The worsening relations between Britain and the Transvaal made it necessary to ensure that Germany did not support the Boers. Germany's goodwill was secured in 1898 by an agreement on the future division of Portugal's colonies in Africa. Portugal's severe financial difficulties, amongst other things, made it seem likely that she would have to relinquish Angola and Mozambique. Germany's share of the spoils would represent a step towards realising her idea of a Central African empire, while the main advantage for Britain was that Germany officially renounced any concern in the affairs of the Transvaal.

QUIT!—PRO QUO?

J. B. "GO AWAY! GO AWAY!!"
FRENCH ORGAN GRINDER. "EH? WHAT YOU GIVE ME IF I GO?"
J. B. "I'LL GIVE YOU SOMETHING IF YOU DON'T!!"

Punch cartoon.

In the Boer War (1899–1902) the British settlers, supported by the Imperial government in London, fought the two Boer republics of the Transvaal and the Orange Free State. The war proved far more difficult to win than expected. According to Kipling, it taught the British 'no end of a lesson', and certainly it dented 'jingo imperialism' in Britain. The continental press rejoiced at every setback to British arms, revealing how unpopular Britain, the leading imperial Power in the world, had become. Her European rivals even discussed schemes for a 'Continental League' directed against her, though British seapower acted as a powerful deterrent to such projects.

In the period 1900–1914 Africa ceased to be an object of serious rivalry amongst the Great Powers. The main exception was North Africa, but even here the rivalry took a different form from that of previous decades. Germany twice challenged France's position in Morocco (in 1905 and 1911) but it was not for the sake of territorial designs on Morocco itself (see pages 83 and 89). Italy's attempt to seize Tripoli (in Libya) in 1911 led to a conflict with Turkey, but the other Powers did not become involved in it, because they did not want Turkey to be weakened any further.

It is clear that a striking feature of the Scramble for Africa was the assertion of European political influence or control over vast tracts of territory, regardless of its current profitability. In China, on the other hand, a genuine 'economic imperialism' can be observed in this same period.

4 Great Power Rivalries in China

> **KEY ISSUES** Why did the Great Powers compete with each other in China? Why was there no partition?

a) An Overview

For a decade after 1895, the Far East became the main focus of international rivalry. Britain's dominant position in trade with China, that stretched back over half a century, was being challenged by other European states. As the economic competition intensified, the rivalry developed political overtones.

The 'Far Eastern Crisis', as some writers call it, began with China's defeat by Japan in 1895 and ended with Japan's victory over Russia in 1905. The revelation of China's weakness at the earlier date led to a short-lived 'scramble for concessions' by the Great Powers. This was followed by territorial demands. China seemed to be in danger of being partitioned. But the fact that only two of the powers, Russia and Japan, had serious designs on Chinese territory is an important reason why China avoided Africa's fate. During this decade of crisis, Britain attempted to set limits to the growth of Russian influence over

China and signed an alliance with Japan in 1902, after Germany had made plain her unwillingness to restrain Russia. The Russo-Japanese war of 1904–5 ended the decade of rivalry and tension amongst the Powers in the Far East.

b) Economic Motivations

The main interest of Britain, France and Germany in China was economic. Certainly, from a geographical viewpoint, they had no strategic interest in this distant part of the world. Yet although it seems clear that trade and investment were the dominant motives for the western Powers' involvement, the trade statistics do not seem to justify all the trouble and effort involved in opening up China to western penetration. The explanation is that China had a population of over 400 million and therefore constituted a vast potential market for manufactured goods. It was this that made the Powers persevere. As late as 1898, a British minister described China as 'the most hopeful place of the future for the commerce of our country'. But even though Britain had about 70 per cent of China's trade, the reality was that her dealings with China represented only about 3 per cent of her total trade in 1885.

On the other hand, in the 1880s China did seem to offer good investment opportunities for European capital. To western eyes, China was ripe for modernisation. As late as 1880 she had no railways and few modern industries or public utilities, such as gas or water companies. Western business firms and banking interests therefore became engaged in a battle for contracts and 'concessions' for mining rights or railway construction. This commercial competition gave a political dimension to the rivalry of the Powers because success in securing economic concessions was seen as a reflection of the political influence that each Power exerted in Peking (today's Beijing). This is shown by the comment made by a British minister in 1898 about a tussle over a railway concessions: 'We are really fighting a battle for prestige rather than for material gain'.

c) Russia and Japan

In the case of Russia and Japan, however, political considerations went far beyond mere prestige. Although the main objective of the Russians was to establish an economic preponderance in Manchuria (see the map on page 55) to assist Russia's industrial development, its realisation depended on establishing political control over this northerly province of China.

Japan's response to western imperialism had been to embark on a policy of modernisation, to take advantage of western ideas and technology. By the 1890s she possessed a modern navy and a reorganised army. In 1894 she felt strong enough to back her claims over Korea, a Chinese dependency, by force. She rapidly secured control of the sea between Korea and north China and occupied parts of mainland China as well as Korea.

Japan's sudden and unexpected defeat of China in the war of 1894–95, however, transformed the situation in the Far East. Japan was clearly now a force to be reckoned with. In fact the Russians were so alarmed at Japan's territorial gains in southern Manchuria, on which Russia herself had designs, that they insisted on a moderation of Japan's demands in the peace treaty. Japan was thus obliged to return some territory to China, in exchange for a larger financial indemnity. Russia's plan was to create a 'special relationship' with China by posing as her friend and saviour against the Japanese; and, in return for a large loan, she obtained valuable economic concessions in Manchuria.

d) The Scramble for China

The war of 1894–95 not only revealed China's weakness but also made her heavily dependent on foreign loans. The result was a 'scramble for concessions', which at times bordered on the absurd. When this 'midsummer madness' had abated in 1898, Britain, for example, had acquired concessions to build 2,800 miles of railways – of which only a few hundred miles had been constructed by 1907! But it also had its more serious side. Russia secured important privileges, including the right to build a railway across Manchuria, greatly reducing the distance from Siberia to Vladivostok. The other Powers also obtained railway and mining concessions. Each nation seemed to be carving out a 'sphere of interest', a trend accentuated by the move towards demanding exclusive privileges for that nation in its sphere. While Russia was attempting to dominate northern China, especially Manchuria, France was most active in the south, adjacent to her empire in Indo-China. Meanwhile Britain, traditionally the advocate of a free trade ('Open Door') policy, was seeking to preserve her long-established position in central China, especially the Yangtze basin. Her most serious competitor here was Germany, whose main area of activity was Shantung province in the north-east. By 1898, therefore, the partition of China into spheres of economic interest seemed to be imminent.

How did China avoid Africa's fate of being partitioned? One factor was that China was a unitary state with a dynasty and a sense of nationhood that Africa lacked. The Chinese authorities also attempted to weaken the trend towards 'spheres' by granting concessions that cut across them. Another factor was the treaty port system. By the 1890s, Europeans could trade at over 30 treaty ports and also enjoyed reasonable access to the interior. In short, political control was not necessary for the sake of trade.

From the European point of view there were two other consider-

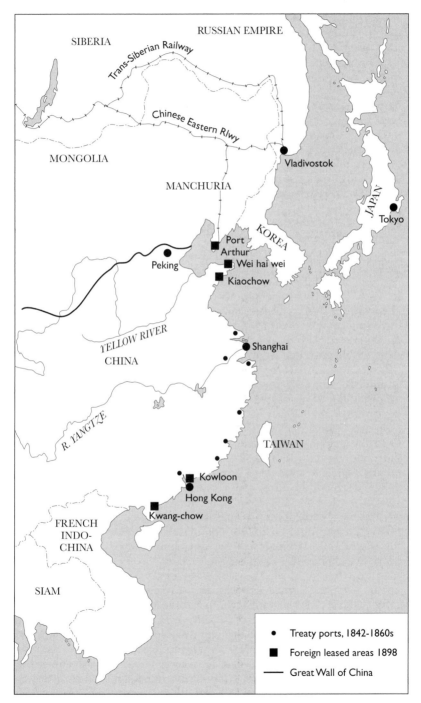

The great powers, Japan and China in the late nineteenth century.

ations that operated against partition. First, the realisation dawned that they might lose more than they gained from it. The fact was that there were only two 'plums' (Manchuria and the Yangtze) to be shared amongst four Powers. The second consideration was the British government's refusal to yield to the clamour of British mercantile interests to create an exclusively British zone in central China because, as was said, 'We are not prepared to undertake the immense responsibility of governing what is practically a third of China'. India was more than enough of a headache without adding to such burdens. The British government therefore, encouraged by an American declaration in favour of the Open Door policy, began successful negotiations with her western rivals to give up demands for exclusive rights in their spheres of interest. With Russia, who refused to give up her privileges in Manchuria, the best the British could do was to secure an agreement in 1899 that eased tension but accepted the spheres concept for railway construction.

e) The Boxer Rebellion and its Impact

In 1900 the Boxer rebellion (organised by the Society of the Harmonious Fists) broke out. Anti-foreigner agitation and riots, including attacks on Europeans and their property, swept through north-eastern China. The most dramatic event was the seven-week siege of the foreign legations, or embassies, in Peking. European rivalry was almost forgotten – temporarily. An international force advanced cautiously on the capital and relieved the legations in August 1900. In reprisal for the atrocities, Peking was subjected to an orgy of rape and pillage, and punitive expeditions were sent to various parts of north China.

In the course of the Boxer rebellion, much damage was done to the railway system in Manchuria. In retaliation the Russian government decided to tighten its grip on the province. Large numbers of troops were employed in suppressing Boxers and 'bandits'. In early 1901 it was learned that Russia had obtained virtual political, as well as economic, control over Manchuria. It seemed only a matter of time before Russia would be able to dominate Peking. One way to prevent this was to enlist German support, as Chamberlain, Britain's Colonial Secretary, suggested in September 1900:

1 I am personally unable to believe in the reform of the Chinese Empire
   as a whole or in the permanent maintenance of its territorial integrity.
   Unless Russia breaks up from internal difficulties, of which there is no
   present sign, I believe she will ultimately secure Northern China, and
5 that the 'Open Door' will be a mere name so far as this part of the
   Chinese Empire is concerned. It is certain that we are not strong
   enough by ourselves to prevent her from accomplishing such an annexation, and both in China and elsewhere it is in our interest that

Germany should throw herself across the path of Russia ... The clash
10 of German and Russian interests, whether in China or Asia Minor,
would be guarantee for our safety.

I think then our policy clearly is to encourage good relations
between ourselves and Germany, as well as between ourselves and
Japan and the United States ... We should, without urging it, let it be
15 known that we shall put no obstacle in the way of German expansion
in Shantung, nor in the way of the gratification of Japan's ambition in
Korea. But, in return, we should obtain written assurances recognising
our claim to predominant interest and influence in the Yang-Tse Valley.
We are not likely ever to want to take possession of any territory in
20 the interior ourselves; but we ought to try for some understanding
which will keep off all others, and make it easy to maintain the 'Open
Door' in at least this, the most important portion of the Chinese
Empire.

In October 1900 the Germans signed an Agreement on China with
Britain. To the British, the Germans had committed themselves to
help defend the *status quo* throughout China, as the terms of the
treaty seemed to imply:

1 Her Britannic Majesty's Government and the Imperial German
Government ... have agreed to observe the following principles in
regard to their mutual policy in China:
1. It is a matter of joint and permanent international interest that the
5 ports on the rivers and littoral of China should remain free and open
to trade ... for the nationals of all countries without distinction; and the
two governments agree ... to uphold the same for all Chinese territory
as far as they can exercise influence.
2. [The two governments] will ... direct their policy towards maintain-
10 ing undiminished the territorial condition of the Chinese Empire.
3. In case of another Power making use of the complications in China
in order to obtain under any form whatever such territorial advantages,
the two Contracting Parties reserve to themselves to come to a preliminary understanding as to the eventual steps to be taken for the pro-
15 tection of their own interests in China.
4. The two Governments will communicate this Agreement to the
other Powers ... and will invite them to accept the principles recorded
in it.
AGREEMENT between Germany and Great Britain relative to China. 16
20 October, 1900.

But British expectations of German support were dashed in March
1901 when Germany made plain her 'absolute indifference' to the
fate of Manchuria, which, she claimed, was outside the scope of the
agreement. Japan was more forthcoming, because Russia still refused
to concede to her the same predominance in Korea that Russia was
now establishing in Manchuria.

In 1902 an Anglo-Japanese Alliance was signed. It recognised Japan's special interests in Korea while supporting the integrity of China. The two allies agreed to aid each other if one of them was attacked by two or more Powers. Strengthened by this assurance of support against a Franco-Russian combination, Japan was able to take a firm line in her negotiations with Russia. When these proved inconclusive, Japan launched a surprise attack against Russian forces in the Far East in February 1904. The war ended in 1905 after sweeping Japanese victories both on land and at sea.

The Russo-Japanese war brought to an end the possibility of Russian domination of northern China. The main threat to China's political independence was thereby removed and her territorial integrity ceased to be an issue of major concern to the Great Powers. For the European Powers, therefore, the Far East ceased to be a source of serious tension.

f) Conclusion

The activities of the Powers in China provide a useful illustration of at least two aspects of imperialism. Firstly, the growing competitiveness for economic advantages turned into a form of political rivalry. Western imperialism in China consequently gave the appearance of being a battle for prestige rather than tangible economic benefits. Secondly, and somewhat paradoxically, the main interest of the European Powers (with the possible exception of Russia) remained nevertheless the exploitation of the commercial and financial opportunities that China offered. In contrast to Africa, where the European states acquired vast tracts of territory, the activities of the western Powers in the Far East can best be described as 'economic imperialism'.

5 Explanations of Imperialism

> **KEY ISSUE** What factors motivated the upsurge of imperial activity?

a) Economic Interpretations

An English radical, J A Hobson, writing in 1902, asserted that imperialism was nothing less than a conspiracy promoted by financiers for their own enrichment. That Hobson should suspect that sinister forces lay behind the annexation of tropical lands is understandable. As he noted, the volume of trade between Britain and these new colonies was small and its profits low. By contrast, Britain's capital investments overseas had greatly increased since 1870 – and Hobson drew the conclusion that Britain acquired colonies to protect this capital investment. Yet his conclusions are no longer convincing. The statistics now available do indeed show that large amounts of British capital were invested abroad, but only a very small proportion went to the territories which subsequently became colonies. Most of it went to the Americas, Australia or old colonies such as India. Hobson was therefore in error in believing that a causal link existed between the acquisition of new colonies and the large increase in overseas investment.

Partial support for the Hobson thesis came in the early-1990s from Peter Cain and Anthony Hopkins, who argued the importance of 'gentlemanly capitalism' ('an alliance ... between the City, southern investors and the landed interest') in producing African partition. They showed that governments were more influenced by the financiers of the City of London (men of the same social and educational elite as the politicians) than by northern industrialists. These were the men who had financial interests abroad, sometimes in Africa, and who encouraged the politicians to raise the Union Jack to protect that investment. It is a challenging idea, though one which sometimes fails to fit all the facts.

Another theorist whose ideas now seem inadequate is the Russian Communist leader Lenin. Writing in 1916–17, he linked imperialism with 'monopoly capitalism'. Once capitalism had matured, the banks controlled both manufacturing industry and governments; and, in their endless search for higher profits, the financiers directed governments to partition Africa to secure valuable raw materials. Yet his views about the nature of capitalism seem inappropriate. Even in France and Britain, monopolies were not nearly as powerful as Lenin insisted, and in industrially backward states, like Russia and Italy, governments were far less influenced by financiers. More fundamentally, Lenin's interpretation is logically flawed. He clearly dates the emergence of 'monopoly finance capitalism' at about 1900. Since he asserts that this was the motive force behind imperialism, it cannot logically be used to explain colonial acquisitions made *before* that date – as most of them were

Yet notions of 'economic imperialism' are by no means dead. In the late nineteenth century, European commercial and financial interests were active throughout the world – in the Far East, Latin America, North America, the Near East and Africa – and trading conditions undoubtedly became increasingly competitive. Industrialisation in Germany and France led to an increase in the output of manufactured goods, while the so-called 'Great Depression' of 1873–96 signified a fall in demand for such products. Hence there was a search for markets for manufactures.

Conditions for Britain were undoubtedly difficult. In the 1880s, British chambers of commerce were talking in terms of a 'crisis of over-production'. The problem for British manufacturers was aggravated because, while Britain clung to free trade, Germany and France adopted protective tariffs. Britain's domestic market and also her colonial markets were open to her rivals, but these rivals proceeded to introduce discriminatory duties against British goods. In the 1890s, when French tariffs were greatly increased, British merchants warned the government that 'Free Trade abroad and prosperity at home were inextricably bound up with imperial expansion'. Several historians see a causal link, in Britain's case, between imperialism and the search to defend trade. Prime Minister Lord Salisbury justified annexing some areas on the grounds that 'we only desire territory because we desire commercial freedom'. This view was expressed quite explicitly by a British official: 'We are forced to extend our direct political influence over a large part of Africa to secure a fair field and no favour for our commerce'. Pressure from German merchants was also one factor that explains Bismarck's sudden interest in Africa in the mid-1880s. By 1890, however, political considerations were foremost, as shown by his remark 'my map of Africa lies in Europe'.

b) Non-Economic Explanations

Many historians are sceptical about the relevance of universal economic theories to explain late-nineteenth-century imperialism. They give greater emphasis to political factors to explain expansion. Increasing attention is also being paid to the 'peripheral' situation – the role of the non-European societies themselves.

Colonial rivalries can be regarded as a transference on to a world stage of the Great Power rivalries that had mostly been confined to Europe and the Near East from 1815 to 1870. It was obviously safer to play out these rivalries in distant lands than in Europe itself. A contemporary observer remarked that 'the great powers are dividing up the continent of Africa ... in the same manner that they would partition countries such as Poland'. The well-established system of conference diplomacy was also applied to the new rivalries in Africa in the form of the Berlin Conference of 1884–85. Contemporaries were very conscious of Great Power competition in Africa. The French politician Jules Ferry likened it to 'a steeplechase moving headlong towards an unknown destination, accelerating as if propelled by its own speed'. This competitiveness encouraged the tendency towards 'preclusive' imperialism – annexing territory, not because it was valuable economically, but merely to forestall a rival.

Imperialism was also closely linked to prestige. Colonies came to be regarded as status symbols. Great Power status, previously measured in terms of population, military capacity and industrial strength, now came to include overseas possessions. Caprivi, Bismarck's successor, said many Germans believed that 'once we came into possession of colonies, then purchased an atlas and coloured the continent of Africa blue, we would become a great people'. The acquisition of Tunisia by France in 1880–81 was hailed as a sign that 'France is recovering her position as a great power'.

In the 1890s public opinion in Britain and elsewhere became an added force behind imperial expansion. 'Jingoism', an assertive form of nationalism, was encouraged (if not promoted) by the popular press. For example, the *Daily Mail* capitalised on 'the depth and volume of public interest in Imperial questions' of its one million readers. In France, where public opinion had been largely apathetic to imperialism before the 1890s, nationalism allegedly made many Frenchmen imperialists. Colonial societies and commercial pressure groups naturally took advantage of this mood to push governments into yet more colonial acquisitions.

The influence of Social Darwinism (see page 71) was also felt on attitudes to colonies and native societies. The maxim 'survival of the fittest', when applied to the human rather than animal kingdom, acted as a justification for colonialism. Superior races – the Europeans – were obviously destined to rule over inferior ones. Britain was 'the greatest of governing races the world has ever seen', in Chamberlain's view. The reverse of this expansionist, self-confident feeling was the fear of decadence and decline. Jules Ferry made the point explicitly when he warned that unless France acquired colonies 'we shall take the road leading to decadence – we shall meet the fate of Spain'. Clearly, nationalism was transforming itself into imperialism.

6 The Causes of the Scramble for Africa

KEY ISSUE Why did the partition of Africa occur?

The partition of Africa can be explained, in part, by some of the motives ascribed to imperialism in general. Nevertheless, some historians have searched for a more specific explanation of it. The 'classic' explanation is that offered by Robinson and Gallagher, who argued that British policy in Africa was essentially a defensive reaction to a series of local crises. The main consideration for the British government in these crises was the security of the route to India. Their interpretation of the situation in southern Africa, in which they stressed the crucial importance of the Cape to imperial interests, has been generally accepted. On the other hand, their view that Egypt acted as a catalyst to the partition of tropical Africa has been criticised. Their notion of a 'chain reaction', in which French resentment at the British occupation of Egypt in 1882 activated a latent rivalry in West Africa, is not sound. French expansion from Senegal, which began in 1879, clearly pre-dated the crisis over Egypt.

The view that it was rival claims to the Congo that sparked off partition is more convincing. Firstly, the interests of at least four European states were involved, not just two as in the case of Egypt. Secondly, Bismarck's role in provoking the Scramble is given due prominence in this interpretation since Germany played an active part in the Congo dispute. Thirdly, the creation of a Franco-German front against Britain's attempt to exclude them from the Congo introduced Great Power diplomacy into the situation in Africa. An additional link between the Congo dispute and the partition of Africa is the Berlin Conference of 1884–85, at which the ground rules for partition were laid down as well as a settlement of the Congo issue itself. Taken together, these four factors indicate that rival claims to the Congo played a more important part in initiating the Scramble than the Anglo-French dispute over Egypt.

A third line of enquiry has sought for an explanation of the timing of the Scramble. The key factor in the 1880s was the decline of British 'paramountcy' in Africa. Until the late 1870s, Britain had succeeded in maintaining an informal influence over most of Africa south of the Sahara. In the 1880s this was challenged. Military defeats in Asia and Africa, coinciding with a decline in relative naval power, were interpreted as signs of British weakness. Bismarck concluded that there would not be much resistance to joint Franco-German pressure. He had reason to resent British pretensions to influence over most of Africa. British paramountcy collapsed like a house of cards when she agreed to an international conference. But its collapse left a void. In this unstable situation Africa was 'up for grabs'. Protectorates were being proclaimed over African territory and some mechanism was needed to settle rival claims. The solution was the Berlin Conference. This marked the formal beginning of the partition of Africa.

The Scramble for Africa cannot be explained satisfactorily without some reference to changes taking place in Africa. Imperialism in general is no longer viewed exclusively in terms of economic or political pressures emanating from Europe. The traditional 'Euro-centric' approach is being modified by increasing recognition of the importance of changes at the 'periphery'. Imperialism is therefore increasingly seen as, in part, a response to a series of local crises and changing situations within Africa itself. African historians have contributed greatly to the awareness of these situations.

European governments were at times responding to crises that arose in different parts of Africa. In Egypt, the growth of an Egyptian nationalist movement forced Britain and France to decide between losing influence or intervention. Britain chose the latter, ostensibly to defend the Suez canal. In southern Africa a succession of crises seemed to put at risk strategic interests at the Cape. Most of these crises stemmed from the expansionist drives of European settlers. The French government faced similar problems from expansionists (especially the military) in Algeria and Senegal. In West Africa, problems arose when stable relationships between Europeans and Africans were upset by changes in the nature, or profitability, of existing patterns of trade.

Two general conclusions may be drawn. Firstly, although economic imperialism is of relevance to European activity in Africa, it may be necessary to regard it as a quite separate factor from the European diplomacy of the Scramble. Secondly, the partition stemmed from an interaction between Europeans and Africans; it is not just a question of the impact of Europe on the Dark Continent.

7 Colonial Rivalries and International Relations

> **KEY ISSUE** How were relations between the major Powers affected by colonial expansion?

Colonial rivalries inevitably had a great impact on relations between the Great Powers. Indeed, apart from the Bulgarian crisis of 1885–87, the focal points of international tension were to be found in Africa and the Far East, rather than in Europe, for much of the period from about 1884 to 1904.

a) Britain's Relations with France and Russia

During most of these years Britain's imperial rivalries with France and Russia were the key factor in international relations. Anglo-French relations underwent a dramatic change as a result of colonial rivalry. From 1870 until about 1884, Britain and France had no major quarrels and usually cooperated in international affairs. The next two decades, however, were marked by continual friction, especially in Africa, bringing them to the verge of war. 'Africa', complained Lord Salisbury, 'was created to be the plague of foreign offices'. Rivalry in West Africa certainly impaired Anglo-French relations. The economic interests of Britain and France there seemed themselves too small to justify war, but prestige was the crux of the matter. A local incident could flare up into a crisis if public opinion, inflamed by the press, insisted that 'national honour' was at stake. Both sides engaged in rather reckless 'brinkmanship', raising the spectre of war on the Niger, until the agreement of 1898. By this date the crisis centre had shifted to the Nile.

Britain's refusal to revive the Anglo-French partnership (the Dual Control) after her military intervention in Egypt in 1882 was a severe blow to French pride. French self-esteem would only be satisfied by a British withdrawal from Egypt. Britain, however, was resolved to stay. One reason for this was that Britain regarded signs of Franco-Russian co-operation in the Mediterranean in the 1890s as a serious threat to her strategic interests. France attempted to exert pressure through the Fashoda expedition. Yet in 1898, Britain would have gone to war with France rather than give way.

The Fashoda crisis ended an era of illusions. Good Anglo-French relations had to be based on France's acceptance of Britain's position in Egypt. The important lesson which the French colonialists drew from Fashoda was that France should barter Egypt in exchange for French predominance in Morocco. They would also give up disputed fishery rights in Newfoundland for minor boundary changes in West Africa. This was the basis of the Anglo-French *entente*, or colonial agreement, of 1904 (see the cartoon on page 65). Paradoxically, therefore, acute rivalry in Africa and Asia transformed international relations in the opposite way to what might have been expected. Tensions prepared the way for *better* relations.

The same process is visible in Anglo-Russian relations. Hostility between Britain and Russia was nothing new, and Russian activities and intrigues in regions bordering India in the 1870s and 1880s continued to cause Britain considerable alarm. Now the era of imperial rivalry transferred the focus of the conflict to the Far East. The Franco-Russian Alliance of 1894 was more obviously anti-British in its operation than anti-German. Yet by 1907 Britain and Russia had concluded an *entente*.

b) Germany's Position

The effect of colonial rivalries on Germany's relations with other Powers was rather ambiguous. Germany seemed to use Africa partly as a means to an end – the furtherance of her diplomatic interests in Europe. In Africa Bismarck found opportunities to conciliate France and distract her from the grievance of Alsace-Lorraine. Hence his encouragement of France to take Tunisia in 1881. The thwarting of Italian ambitions there assured Franco-Italian hostility for a decade and induced Italy to join the Triple Alliance. Africa was also fertile ground for Franco-German co-operation against Britain. The British resented his making difficulties over Egypt as a sort of blackmail to secure concessions for Germany elsewhere. In the case of the Congo, Bismarck persuaded France to join Germany in 1884 in opposing Britain's rather dubious treaty with Portugal to exclude French and German interests. However, Germany was not in this period regarded as an undesirable colonial neighbour. The partitions of East Africa in 1886 and 1890 were negotiated in a fairly cordial spirit.

When Bismarck was German Chancellor, colonial conflicts were kept within certain limits. After 1890, however, German overseas policy became much less predictable and restrained, and this ultimately had a damaging effect on Anglo-German relations. German support for the Boers was a source of serious tension, as the affair of the Kruger telegram in 1896 showed (see page 77). The most serious clash in Africa was the clumsy attempt by Germany to provoke a crisis directed against French imperialism in Morocco in 1905 and in 1911 (see pages 83 and 89). This had the effect of strengthening, rather than weakening, Britain's *ententes* with France and Russia. By 1914 indeed the Anglo-French colonial understanding had become almost an alliance.

A MUTUAL SACRIFICE:

OR, L'AUTEL DU LIBRE ÉCHANGE.

A *Punch* cartoon.

c) The Far East: Britain's Alliance with Japan

Great Power rivalries in the Far East also had important effects on international relations. Russia was the only European Power to become involved in war, but her rivalry with Britain resulted in considerable tension. When British hopes of an alliance with Germany to resist Russian expansion in China were dashed, Britain turned to Japan.

In one sense the 1902 Anglo-Japanese alliance marked the end of Britain's 'Splendid Isolation'. She had now abandoned her traditional policy of avoiding 'entangling alliances' in peacetime. The serious implications of the treaty with Japan were voiced by Lord Salisbury: 'It involves a pledge on our part to defend Japanese action in Korea ... against France and Russia ... There is no limit; and no escape. We are pledged to war.' On the other hand, the alliance was restricted in scope: it was a regional pact, limited to the Far East. Some historians have therefore argued that the alliance did not impair Britain's freedom to maintain her isolation from her continental rivals. Yet this is not quite accurate. In 1903 Britain, as the ally of Japan, feared she might become involved in war against France, as the ally of Russia. The commitment to Japan acted consequently as a catalyst to the negotiations for an *entente* with France.

The Russo-Japanese war of 1904–5 did not involve Britain. But Russia's defeat by Japan had serious repercussions for international relations. Russia's prestige suffered a major blow and her military and naval capacity were greatly reduced. The outbreak of revolution in Russia in 1905, in protest against the incompetence of the Tsarist regime, weakened her further. Russia was therefore unable to play her full part as a Great Power in European affairs for several years after 1905. As we shall see, Germany was to take advantage of this. Furthermore, checked in the Far East, Russian ambitions turned back once more to the Balkans.

Imperial rivalries in Africa and Asia were not without their dangers but at least they were played out at a safe distance and did not usually involve questions of security and survival. In 1905, however, the centre of gravity of international affairs returned to Europe when Germany, quite gratuitously, raised the spectre of war against France. In the next chapter we turn to this *Weltpolitik* in action.

Working on Chapter 3

This is a long chapter. Do not be daunted by it. In particular, do not worry if, at least on a first reading, section 3 (on the Scramble for Africa) appears complicated. Be sure to grasp the overall contours of what happened (with the aid of the maps on Africa and China). Also, use the complexity (the events, the 'players', their motives) to test out

Summary Diagram
Colonial Rivalries, 1870–1914

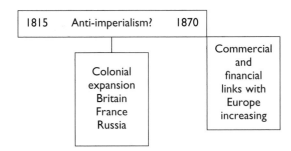

```
┌─────────────────────────────────────────────┐
│ 1815      Anti-imperialism?      1870         │
└───────────────────┬──────────────────┬───────┘
            ┌───────┴───────┐  ┌────────┴────────┐
            │   Colonial    │  │   Commercial    │
            │   expansion   │  │      and        │
            │   Britain     │  │   financial     │
            │   France      │  │   links with    │
            │   Russia      │  │   Europe        │
            │               │  │   increasing    │
            └───────────────┘  └─────────────────┘
```

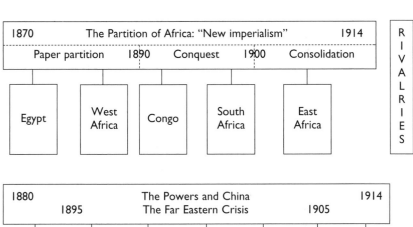

```
┌───────────────────────────────────────────────────────────────┐ ┌───┐
│ 1870       The Partition of Africa: "New imperialism"   1914    │ │ R │
├───────────────────────────────────────────────────────────────┤ │ I │
│   Paper partition    1890    Conquest    1900    Consolidation  │ │ V │
└──┬──────────┬──────────┬──────────┬──────────────┬─────────────┘ │ A │
   │          │          │          │              │               │ L │
┌──┴──┐  ┌────┴───┐  ┌───┴───┐  ┌───┴────┐    ┌────┴───┐          │ R │
│     │  │        │  │       │  │        │    │        │          │ I │
│Egypt│  │ West   │  │Congo  │  │ South  │    │ East   │          │ E │
│     │  │ Africa │  │       │  │ Africa │    │ Africa │          │ S │
└─────┘  └────────┘  └───────┘  └────────┘    └────────┘          └───┘
```

```
┌──────────────────────────────────────────────────────────────────────────────┐
│ 1880                    The Powers and China                    1914           │
│        1895             The Far Eastern Crisis        1905                      │
└──┬────────┬────────┬─────────┬─────────────┬─────────┬─────────┬───────────────┘
```

| Concession-hunting 1880s | Sino-Japanese War 1894–5 | Scramble for concessions 1895–8 | Territorial claims 1897–8 | Boxer rebellion Anglo-German Agreement 1900 | Anglo-Japanese Alliance 1902 | Russo-Japanese War 1904–5 |

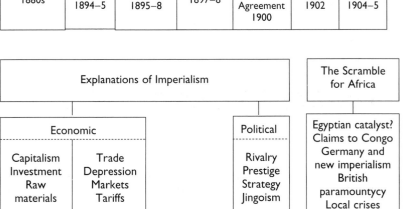

```
┌─────────────────────────────────────────────────┐  ┌──────────────────┐
│            Explanations of Imperialism            │  │  The Scramble    │
│                                                   │  │   for Africa     │
└──────────────────────┬────────────────┬──────────┘  └────────┬─────────┘
```

Economic		Political	Egyptian catalyst?
Capitalism Investment Raw materials	Trade Depression Markets Tariffs	Rivalry Prestige Strategy Jingoism	Claims to Congo Germany and new imperialism British paramountycy Local crises

the theories that seek to explain the Partition. Remember that a theory, however seemingly logical, is redundant if it does not explain real events. One part of your notes could compare imperial rivalry in Africa and China. What similarities were there, and what differences? Pay particular attention to the concluding section, and be clear in your own mind about the consequences imperialism had for Great Power relations.

Answering structured and essay questions on Chapter 3

Questions on this topic tend to focus on one of four issues: the causes of imperialism; the reasons for the partition of Africa; the nature of colonial activities; and the effects of colonial rivalries on international relations. The commonest questions are those that ask for an explanation of imperialism or of the Scramble for Africa.

Study the following structured question:

a) (i) What are the main economic theories that have been put forward to explain the Scramble for Africa? (5 marks) (ii) What are their strengths and weaknesses? (5 marks)
b) (i) What non-economic theories have been advanced to account for the Scramble? (5 marks) (ii) What are their strengths and weaknesses? (5 marks)
c) To what extent were the European Powers motivated by economic concerns in their partition of Africa? (20 marks)

Remember that c) gives you as many marks as a) and b) combined. It gives you a chance to be more analytical – i.e. to relate theories to what actually happened and to reach a balanced conclusion. Remember to refer to different parts of Africa, for instance mentioning the importance of diamonds in south Africa.

Consider also the following essay questions:

1. Why was the late nineteenth century an 'age of imperialism'?
2. 'That flag followed the trade.' Discuss this explanation of the 'new imperialism'.
3. 'The motives for the partition of Africa were diplomatic rather than economic.' Discuss this statement.
4. 'Non-economic factors were of little importance in bringing about the African partition.' How valid is this statement?
5. Explain and illustrate the growing interest of the European powers in China in the late nineteenth century.
6. In what ways did the 'Scramble for Africa' affect relations between the European Powers during this period?

Remember the importance of defining the terms in each question. For instance, you must define 'imperialism' in question 1. In that way, you can work out exactly what a question means and requires – and you will see that questions which seem very different, e.g. questions 2, 3 and 4, are really very similar, although you will need a different emphasis to answer each of them. Also, be aware of the need to divide the overall questions into smaller sub-questions, on each of which you will have a paragraph. Finally, do not neglect evidence. Every good essay should achieve a balance between interpretations (ideas) and detailed factual information to support those ideas. Many writers on this topic confine themselves to theory – but do not follow their example.

Source-based questions on Chapter 4

1 Great power rivalry in China, 1900

Read carefully the extracts from the Chamberlain Memorandum and the Anglo-German Agreement, given on pages 56–7. Answer the following questions:

a) What was Chamberlain's policy, as described in the first extract, for protecting British interests in China? (5 marks)

b) Were the terms of the Anglo-German Agreement in conformity with Chamberlain's policy? Explain your answer. (10 marks)

c) What were the implications of the fourth point in the Agreement? (3 marks)

d) On what basis could it be argued that the Agreement was hardly worth the paper it was written on? (7 marks)

e) What criticisms could be made of Chamberlain's policy, as described in his Memorandum? (5 marks)

f) Use these sources, and your other knowledge, to estimate the state of relations between Britain, Germany and Russia at this time. (15 marks)

2 Three Cartoons

Examine carefully the cartoons on pages 49, 51 and 65 and answer the following questions:

a) What view of the nature of imperialism is suggested by the first cartoonist (p. 49) through his portrayal of Africa and of the European Powers? What is the significance of the snake in the foreground of the cartoon? (10 marks)

b) What is the attitude of the cartoonist of the 'QUIT! – PRO QUO?' cartoon towards France, as revealed by, i) his choice of characters to represent Britain and France, and ii) the words spoken by the two characters? ('Quid Pro Quo' means, literally 'something for something else', or recompense). Justify your answer. (10 marks)

c) What does the third cartoonist (p. 65) imply about the nature of the *Entente Cordiale*? What is the significance of the laurel wreath in the foreground?

d) Using your knowledge of the period, examine the bias of each cartoonist and estimate how historically accurate the depiction in each cartoon was. (15 marks)

4 *Weltpolitik* and European Tensions, 1890–1911

POINTS TO CONSIDER

This was an important, and crowded, period in international affairs. It is necessary to consider the role of ideas (and images and beliefs and assumptions) in poisoning international relations, but we also have to examine the policies that led to tension and crises. Pay particular attention to Germany, trying to assess the role of key individuals like the Kaiser. Did tensions escalate because of the intentions of the policy-makers? Or were the unintended results of particular policies more important? Try to see each country's actions from several points of view – from that of its own government, from that of its rivals and also from that of the historian (who has knowledge of what particular actions led to).

KEY DATES

1890	Bismarck replaced as Chancellor by Caprivi; Reinsurance Treaty with Russia was not renewed.
1894	Franco-Russian Alliance was ratified.
1898	First German navy bill (second in 1900).
1902	Anglo-Japanese Alliance.
1904	*Entente Cordiale* (Britain and France).
1905	First Moroccan Crisis.
1906	Algeçiras conference; launching of the first Dreadnought.
1907	Anglo-Russian Entente.
1908	Bosnian Crisis.
1911	Agadir (Second Moroccan) Crisis.

1 The Climate of Opinion

> **KEY ISSUES** What were some of the common ideas and assumptions relevant to international affairs around 1900? How significant were they?

The period from about 1880 to 1914 has often been called the 'Age of Imperialism'. In many ways this is a vague phrase, and certainly the word 'imperialism' has been used in too many diverse ways to have any clear meaning. Some employ the term to mean the acquisition of overseas colonies (see Chapter 3), some to denote the domination – political, economic or cultural – of one country over another, and others to signify militarism, the building of bigger and more destructive armed forces. But perhaps the common feature in imperialism is an aggressive mental attitude. The imperialist believes that his nation is superior to others, which are dismissed as inferior and treated accordingly. Such an attitude – a turning outwards onto the international arena of nationalism – may well have been a prime factor in the growth of tension in European affairs and in the origins of the First World War.

a) Social Darwinism

One component in the imperialist world-view was Social Darwinism. This derived from the works of Charles Darwin, whose theory of evolution aroused considerable interest, and sparked off bitter controversy, in the second half of the nineteenth century. His ideas were often tentative and put forward with hesitation; but many of his followers were far more self-confident, and they believed that his theories applied to human societies as well as animals. In particular Herbert Spencer produced a highly simplified version of Darwinism, identifying its main principle as 'the survival of the fittest'. Spencer insisted that countries were like animals and that all had to struggle and fight in order to survive: those who won would grow stronger, while those who lost would decline and fall. What nations could not do was live in peace with each other for long. The stark options were to get stronger or weaker, to progress or regress. War, therefore, was not an evil to be avoided but a means of national evolution. It was inevitable sooner or later. Nations would go to war, just as animals fought, because it was in their nature to do so.

b) The Image of War

The popular idea of war around the turn of the century was of a glorious adventure which would benefit its participants. This view was spread by many means, including popular novels and journalism. Even Herbert Spencer found the British press too much: he gave up reading newspapers because they 'reeked with violence'. War correspondents tended to describe battles as heroic exploits not, as they often really were, bloody massacres. One popular British writer, George Steevens, insisted that war was a 'coming of age' which improved men: indeed it was 'the only quite complete holiday ever invented'! Such views were not confined to journalists. Eminent and cultured men had similar ideas. Nor were they confined to Britons.

In Germany Helmuth von Moltke, the hero of the Franco-Prussian War, expressed common views when he declared:

> War is an element of the divine order of the world. In it are developed the noblest virtues of man: courage and self-denial, fidelity to duty and

the spirit of sacrifice; soldiers give their lives. Without war, the world would stagnate and lose itself in materialism.

As the memory of real war in Europe faded after 1871, so this glorious and highly unrealistic image took its place. Generations of schoolchildren were taught that their highest duty was to die for their country. (Even infants were militarised. A best-selling toy in Britain in 1900 was the 'Dying Boer' which, when squeezed, emitted sounds like the moans of a dying man.) Various leagues militarised youth. We all know that the Boy Scouts, founded in 1908 in Britain, promised to 'Be prepared' – but prepared for what? Their full motto was that they would be prepared 'to die for your country, so that when the time comes you may charge home with confidence, not caring whether you are to be killed or not'. In every major European country but Britain this militarisation of youth was followed by the conscription of large armies – and pressure groups existed to ensure that governments did not allow their country to fall behind the competition. In Germany, for instance, the Naval League attracted over a million members.

c) The Image of Foreigners

Around the start of the twentieth century there was a confident belief that European nations were superior to those of other continents. In addition, there was thought to be a hierarchy among Europeans too. Each European state tended to look pityingly on the citizens of other states for their misfortune in being foreign. And pity often turned to contempt, if not hatred. It was very common for people in one country to stereotype those in another: instead of seeing real human beings, all different, they saw representative figures embodying what they considered to be their nation's characteristics.

Even Leo Tolstoy, one of the great figures in world literature, stereotyped Europeans in his novel *Resurrection* (1899):

1 The Frenchman is self-assured because he regards himself personally
   both in mind and body as irresistibly attractive to men and women. An
   Englishman is self-assured as being a citizen of the best-organised state
   in the world and therefore, as an Englishman, always knows what he
5 should do and knows that all he does as an Englishman is undoubtedly
   correct ... A Russian is self-assured just because he knows nothing and
   does not want to know anything, since he does not believe that anything
   can be known. The German's self-assurance is worst of all, because he
   imagines that he knows the truth – science – which he himself has
10 invented but which is for him the absolute truth.

In Britain, the proprietor of the most popular newspaper of the day, the *Daily Mail*, was determined to give the public what they wanted – which in his view was 'a good hate'. Hence his most popular journalist, George Steevens, presented wildly distorted views of foreigners.

The Chinaman was 'deceitful above all things, and desperately wicked'; the Arab was lazy ('give him half-an-hour and he will take an hour'); and the African 'was satisfied with his proper position of inferiority'. Europeans were also criticised, though the French and German had contrasting faults:

1　Frenchmen do not want to rule – they want to live. The pursuit of life, of laughter, of charming sensations, of intelligent apprehensions, of individual development of character – it may be all the more important, more vital to human existence than the preoccupation, in oneself and
5　others, to make laws and fight. Only this you can say from history and common sense: that if one nation thus abandons the political life while other nations still pursue it, the solitary nation, sooner or later, will suffer from the pressure of the others.
　　Under the Iron Heel ... It needs no customs-house to tell you that you
10　have come to Germany. You are in a new atmosphere – an atmosphere of order, of discipline, of system, rigidly applied to the smallest detail ... You are not a person so much as the object of a direction ... The average German concentrates himself so thoroughly on doing what he is told, that you are bound to wonder how much he could do if he were
15　not told.

Clearly there was more to fear from the German than from the Frenchman, but neither had the qualities to be found in the English, who could act in a disciplined fashion without losing their individual initiative. Often foreigners were caricatured in print as grossly as they were in cartoons (see, for instance, those on pages 49 and 51).

d) Conclusion

Clearly a warlike climate of opinion was developing around 1900: war was presented as glorious and also as inevitable (due to Social Darwinism), and moreover one's enemies were seen as inferior, thus making victory seem assured.

But what significance should be assigned to these ideas and images? It is possible to say, with Norman Stone, that, before the declarations of war in the summer of 1914, war had already broken out 'in men's minds'. Perhaps, therefore, this is a key area for an understanding of the origins of the Great War, especially since, for perhaps the first time in human history, governments in Europe were well aware of public opinion, as mobilised by mass-circulation newspapers.

Yet we should be wary of 'blanket' generalisations. First, it must be said that, though warlike beliefs and assumptions did exist, it is difficult to measure their strength. Certainly not everyone was affected by them, as is shown by the existence of pacifists and peace movements. By concentrating on bellicose sentiments, we may well fail to see them in the perspective of society as a whole. Second, war broke out at a particular time and because of the actions of significant individuals.

Hence the climate of opinion certainly cannot provide a full explanation of what happened. Hence we must turn to the key events that led to a deterioration of international affairs and finally to war.

2 German Diplomacy after Bismarck, 1890–96

> **KEY ISSUE** Why did Germany's position in European affairs deteriorate in this period?

In the six years following Bismarck's fall, German foreign policy lacked a clear sense of direction and her international position was greatly weakened. France and Russia made an alliance, but Germany failed, as a response, to bind Britain more closely to the Triple Alliance. Indeed Anglo-German relations declined dramatically. Germany's leaders lacked the skill to translate ideas into successful policies.

a) The 'New Course'

Bismarck's successor as Chancellor, Caprivi, began a 'New Course' from 1890, deliberately rejecting Bismarck's system. This involved the crucial decision, taken in 1890, not to renew the Reinsurance Treaty of 1887 with Russia (see page 35). This was mainly due to Holstein, a senior official in the foreign ministry who persuaded the Chancellor and the Kaiser that the treaty was incompatible with Germany's commitments to her other allies, especially Austria-Hungary. This decision prepared the ground for the major event of the decade in international affairs – the Franco-Russian Alliance of 1892–94.

France, a democratic Republic, and Russia, ruled by an autocratic Tsar, seem strange bedfellows. A common fear of Germany would be the obvious explanation for their unnatural union. In the early 1890s, however, Russia had no serious conflict with Germany and wanted to renew the Reinsurance Treaty. The initiative for the alliance came from France who, for the sake of security from a German attack, wanted a military agreement with Russia. The French proposals did not appeal to the Tsar's more conservative ministers, but Russia needed loans from France now that the Germans were unwilling to grant them (see page 33). Two separate agreements were made – a political *entente* in 1891, followed by a military convention a year later. The political agreement was anti-British in intent, aligning France with Russia in imperial disputes. In the military convention, France and Russia promised mutual support if either were attacked by Germany, and immediate mobilisation in response to mobilisation by one or more of the Triple Alliance Powers. France had to wait until 1894 for the Tsar's confirmation, and the signing of a full-scale alliance.

The Franco-Russian Alliance brought to an end the Bismarckian system by which Germany had directed the affairs of Europe for two decades. France had now broken out from the 'quarantine' imposed on her by Bismarck. The ultimate significance of the Alliance was not lost on Berlin: Germany now faced the prospect of a war on two fronts. Her response was the Schlieffen Plan.

The Schlieffen Plan

Count Alfred von Schlieffen was Chief of the German General Staff in 1891–1905. It was his job to plan an appropriate military strategy to combat the Franco-Russian combination. His idea was that Germany should avoid fighting on two fronts simultaneously, since this would necessitate a dangerous division of German resources. If war broke out, Germany, he decided, should deliver a knock-out blow against France in the west in six weeks. Then German forces should move to the eastern front to fight the larger but more slowly mobilising Russian army. The Schlieffen Plan was worked out in the 1890s and was complete by 1906. It was a scheme to which Germany became committed.

The potential danger to Germany from the Franco-Russian Alliance could have been partially offset by the conclusion of an Anglo-German alliance. British naval power and German military strength would have made a formidable combination. Moreover, Germany could expect to enlist British support against Russia for the defence of Austro-Hungarian interests in the Balkans. Yet although an alliance with Britain was a major element of Caprivi's 'New Course', the German leaders failed to secure it.

The prospects for an alliance seemed good in the early 1890s when cordiality was the keynote of Anglo-German relations. In the Heligoland-Zanzibar Treaty of 1890 (see page 49), Germany made generous concessions to satisfy British claims in East Africa. Another factor was Britain's rivalry with France and Russia. The Germans, however, failed to capitalise on this mood. They were perhaps complacent, believing that sooner or later Britain would have to seek an alliance. One obstacle, however, was the aversion of Lord Salisbury (who doubled up as prime minister and foreign sectretary in (1887–92 and 1895–1900), to a formal alliance. His wanted 'the advantages of friendship without the encumbering engagements of an alliance'.

An opportunity for creating closer ties with Britain arose in 1894 when the then British Prime Minister, Lord Rosebery, reassured the Austrians of his determination to defend Constantinople. But to ensure that Britain had to deal with Russia only, he required a commitment from Germany that she would keep France in check. In

Berlin, however, this was regarded as a clumsy British trick. Caprivi wrongly suspected that Britain wanted a free hand to attack Russia whenever she chose, leaving Germany to face the risk of war with France. Hence the German government lost a real chance to strengthen the links between Britain and the Triple Alliance. They had miscalculated, believing Britain needed Germany more than Germany needed Britain. Soon relations between the two countries were to deteriorate.

-Profile-

KAISER WILHELM II (who lived from 1859–1941 and reigned in 1888–1918)

Wilhelm was born in 1859, the eldest son of Crown Prince Frederick and his wife Victoria, the daughter of Britain's Queen Victoria. It was a difficult breach birth: the umbilical cord was wrapped round the neck of the baby, so that his brain was probably starved of oxygen for a short time, and his left arm was ripped out of its socket. It seems that he was scarred psychologically, but not so much by his withered left arm as by the fact that his parents made him undergo painful exercises – and even more painful electric shock treatment – to improve it. He was never allowed to forget his disability in his formative years (even though he later disguised it very well, as in the portrait on the cover of this book), and he compensated by an aggressive masculinity. He was also confused about his identity – half-German and half-British – and developed a strange love-hate relationship with Britain.

Several historians believe that Wilhelm was disturbed mentally. Bismarck remarked that he was 'like a balloon. If you do not hold fast to the string, you never know where he will be off to.' A friend described him on a sea-voyage in 1903 wandering about the ship 'as if in a dream-world, often his face completely distorted with rage. Sometimes he appeared to have lost discipline over himself entirely … Pale, ranting wildly, looking restlessly about him and piling lie upon lie, he made such a terrible impression on me that I still cannot get over it.'

This was the man who became Kaiser in 1888 and dismissed Bismarck two years later. Some see him as a positive menace in international relations, as the man who – more than any other single person – was responsible for the Great War. Others, however, call him a 'shadow emperor', a man who did not work hard enough to rule as well as reign. As Bismarck remarked, he wanted 'every day to be a Sunday' (a day of rest). According to this school of thought, responsibility for the war that broke out in 1914 lies elsewhere.

It is important to remember that Wilhelm II possessed great political power. A complex character whose moods were liable to change very rapidly and violently, he sometimes ignored official business but occasionally intervened decisively to influence policy. Hence while he was Kaiser it is difficult to say who controlled German policy. He was certainly a powerful voice at times, but on the whole power was diffused. The Kaiser, the Chancellor, the foreign minister, foreign ministry officials, and army and navy chiefs – all these played a role in determining German foreign policy. Unlike in Bismarck's day, the aims of German diplomacy were now seldom defined or clear priorities established.

Wilhelm abdicated in 1918 and spent the rest of his life as an exile in Holland.

b) Germany 'The Troublemaker'

After Caprivi's resignation in 1894, the German government, despairing of Britain as an ally, turned to alternative lines of policy. The first was an attempt to turn the clock back to 1890 by seeking agreement with Russia. Yet, despite the conclusion of a commercial treaty favourable to Russian agrarian interests, the Tsar would not jettison the alliance with France. Even so, Russo-German relations were quite cordial for some years, helped by the fact that the new Tsar, Nicholas II, got on well with the Kaiser, his cousin.

Having failed to secure an agreement with Russia, the Germans tried a different course. This amounted to a policy of meddling almost at random in colonial issues, such as boundary disputes in the Sudan, the future of the Portuguese colonies in Africa, and doing so with a bullying and offensive tone. Even when Germany had reasonable grounds for her actions, her style of diplomacy caused considerable offence as well as puzzlement at her motives. This was particularly the case in London. Salisbury said in 1895 that 'The conduct of the German Emperor is very mysterious and difficult to explain. There is a danger of his going completely off his head.'

The culmination of this type of diplomacy was the affair of the 'Kruger Telegram' in 1896. The Jameson raid, an armed attack (initiated by Cecil Rhodes, using British South Africa Company police) to incite an uprising in Johannesburg against the Boers, was an illegal act against the Transvaal state. As thousands of Germans were active in the commercial life of the country, it was quite proper for the German government to express concern. Their manner of proceeding, however, was very clumsy. Once Berlin was informed that the raid had not been approved by the British government, the matter might have been allowed to rest. Instead, the Germans invited French and Russian co-operation against Britain, hoping that this sort of pressure would induce her to join the Triple Alliance. When the French and Russians refused, the Kaiser sent a telegram, to Kruger, the Boer President, supporting the independence of the Transvaal. The British press treated the Kaiser's action as a gross interference in Britain's imperial affairs. According to the German ambassador in London, 'If the [British] government had wished for war ... it would have had the whole of public opinion behind it'.

c) Germany's Foreign Relations around 1896

Anglo-German relations, so cordial in 1890, were now frosty. But it was not only Anglo-German relations that had deteriorated since Bismarck's fall. In 1890 Berlin had been the focal point of European diplomacy, with the Triple Alliance and the Reinsurance Treaty. By 1896, however, France was the ally of Russia, and Germany's international position was much less secure. Clearly, German diplomacy since 1890 had been a conspicuous failure. Yet even now the German government had no intention of pursuing policies of restraint and caution.

3 *Weltpolitik* and the End of British Isolation, 1897–1904

> **KEY ISSUES** What was meant by *Weltpolitik*? What motives lay behind it and why did it alienate Britain?

a) The Motives behind *Weltpolitik*

In 1897, Germany embarked on a 'World Policy' (*Weltpolitik*). This was a conscious rejection of Bismarck's policies, which had been centred on Europe. The emphasis was now on expansion, especially overseas expansion, and on the creation of a big navy.

Weltpolitik did not have a very precise meaning, but it is a convenient term to sum up the expansionist phase of German policy that began in the late 1890s. 1897 is usually regarded as marking its beginning. In that year the Kaiser made two important changes in his ministers. Bülow was appointed to the foreign ministry and Admiral von Tirpitz to head the navy office. The latter appointment, followed by German Naval Bills in 1898 and 1900, signified that Germany was to begin the construction of a powerful battle fleet. The role of the new foreign minister, Bülow, was twofold. Firstly, he was to foster good relations with Britain while the German fleet was in its infancy. Secondly, he had to improve Germany's position on the world stage and satisfy the German people's craving for 'a place in the sun' – a tropical empire. The Kaiser, himself an enthusiast for expansion, said in 1898, 'Germany has great tasks to accomplish outside the narrow boundaries of old Europe'.

What these 'great tasks' were is not very obvious. As Germany's army commander remarked around this time: 'We are supposed to pursue *Weltpolitik*. If only we knew what it was supposed to mean.' Whether its content or ultimate objectives were ever clearly defined is still a matter of debate. Contemporary observers, as well as modern historians, were uncertain how to interpret *Weltpolitik*. Eyre Crowe, a Foreign Office official, commented on it in 1907 in these terms:

1 Either Germany is definitely aiming at a general political hegemony and maritime ascendancy, threatening the independence of her neighbours and ultimately the existence of England; or Germany, free from any such clear-cut ambition and thinking for the present merely of using her legit-
5 imate position and influence as one of the leading powers … is seeking to promote her foreign commerce … and create fresh German interests all over the world wherever and whenever a peaceful opportunity offers, leaving it to an uncertain future to decide whether the occurrence of great changes in the world may not some day assign to
10 Germany a larger share of direct political action over regions not now part of her dominions without that violation of the established rights of other countries which would be involved in any such action under existing political conditions.

Behind the pursuit of *Weltpolitik* there lay a vague longing to be a World Power. Many Germans were conscious of their nation's growing power. Second only to Britain as the world's largest trading and commercial nation, Germany also ranked second (after the USA) in the world as a great industrial nation. Yet this economic strength was not reflected in the size of her overseas empire, and this was a grievance to many. Alongside the 'world empires' of the USA, Russia and the British Empire, Germany's territories seemed inadequate. Eyre Crowe believed that:

1 the dream of a colonial empire had taken deep hold on the German imagination. Emperor, statesmen, journalists, … economists … and the whole mass of … public opinion continue with one voice to declare: We must have real colonies … and we must have a fleet and coaling
5 stations to keep together the colonies we are bound to acquire.

It was pressures such as these which induced Bülow to assert: 'We can't do anything other than carry out *Weltpolitik*'.

Yet most historians are not fully satisfied with this explanation.

They see Germany's unstable and old-fashioned political system, dominated by the Kaiser, as an important reason for the adoption of *Weltpolitik*. The course of German foreign policy after 1897 is seen, at one level, as a response to democracy and socialism.

Industrial growth promoted the wealth of the middle classes and also the size of the working classes – and both of these groups wanted to achieve political power. Particularly worrying was the rise of the German Socialist Party (SPD). It won 35 seats in the Reichstag in 1890 (out of 397); but this number rose to 56 in 1898. The old arrangement therefore, where power lay above all with the Kaiser and the landowners, seemed unlikely to last. Hence it can be argued that the traditional ruling classes resorted to 'diversionary tactics' to distract opinion from domestic tensions and problems by pursuing prestige on a world scale. Bülow said: 'Only a successful foreign policy can help to reconcile, rally and unite.' A large and successful navy might even transform the Kaiser into a popular hero. In short, imperialism was a substitute for unwanted social change – hence the phrase 'social imperialism'. Or at least *Weltpolitik* was expected to rally the 'patriotic forces' – Conservatives, National Liberals and the Catholic Party – behind the government. According to this view, the primary motivation behind German foreign policy was the need to stabilise domestic politics.

It seems likely that there was no masterplan behind *Weltpolitik*. It was a strange mixture of reasonable aspirations and some justified claims, combined with ill-defined objectives. Perhaps for this reason, the achievements of German diplomacy in the period from 1897 to 1904 were rather limited. Kiaochow was obtained from China as a naval base in 1897 and the Shantung province claimed as Germany's 'sphere of interest' for economic exploitation. She purchased a group of islands in the Pacific (the Carolines, Marshalls and Marianas) from Spain in 1898. Negotiations with Britain over the future of Portugal's empire in Africa seemed to offer the prospect of more substantial colonial gains which might have made a reality of German aspirations to dominate 'middle Africa' (*Mittelafrika*). The British government, however, played a double game by averting the bankruptcy of Portugal on which German hopes were based. A joint Anglo-German blockade of Venezuela, which had defaulted on its foreign debts, in 1902–03 was a sign of the willingness of the two governments to co-operate; but the bombardment of a port by the German flotilla created a storm in the British press, forcing the government to abandon the blockade.

b) Anglo-German Relations

The British press also frustrated the attempt by the Conservative government in England to co-operate with Germany in the Berlin-Baghdad railway scheme. The British government was willing to support this ambitious project, which was designed to open up the

Near East to European (especially German) economic penetration, on condition that certain key sections of the line were under international control. It was the pressure of 'this anti-German fever', as Lansdowne, Salisbury's successor as foreign secretary, called it, that obliged the government to withdraw its support in 1903.

Clearly, public opinion in Britain and Germany was becoming a significant factor in Anglo-German relations. Economic rivalry between the two great manufacturing and trading nations was keenly felt, aggravated by disputes over tariff policies. In Germany, 'anglophobia' (hatred of England) reached its height during the Boer War, 1899–1902. In Britain, 'Germanophobia' became quite pronounced in the 1900s. (In 1894 William Le Queux's best-selling novel, *The Great War in England in 1897*, had depicted a Franco-Russian invasion of England which was repulsed with the aid of Germany. But since then there had been a complete turn-around: Germany was now popularly depicted as the aggressor in British popular fiction. Le Queux jumped on the bandwagon, with *The Invasion of 1910*.) This was partly a result of the second Navy Law of 1900, which doubled the size of the projected German fleet, giving rise to fears for Britain's naval supremacy.

The growing antagonism had more serious implications for Germany than Britain. An important element in German policy was to allay British suspicions while the German navy was being expanded. The Kaiser had done his best by successful visits to England. Bülow, on the other hand, was quite convinced that Britain's imperial rivalries with Russia and, to a lesser extent, with France must inevitably lead to war. It therefore followed that it would be a mistake for Germany to align herself with Britain and thereby antagonise Russia. All Germany had to do was to wait for the inevitable conflict, and then extract a high price for her favours. Hence Bülow's delight at the Fashoda crisis of 1898 (see page 50) and, early in 1904, at the outbreak of the Russo-Japanese war. Britain, he assumed, would become involved as the ally of Japan. Bülow's policy had had a certain logic to it, but it also contained a fatal flaw. It made no allowance for Britain resolving her imperial rivalries without war.

By the turn of the century leading Conservative ministers, especially Chamberlain, the very influential colonial secretary, shared Bülow's pessimistic appraisal of Britain's situation in the world. 'Splendid Isolation' seemed outmoded for 'the weary Titan' staggering under the 'too vast orb of his fate', as Chamberlain put it. His solution, pursued from 1898 to 1901, was an alliance with Germany. Yet it made no sense for Germany to antagonise Russia in the Far East where, for the most part, her activities did not threaten the interests of Germany or her allies. As a result, disappointed with Germany, British ministers slowly came to appreciate more fully the value of Japan as an ally to check Russian ambitions in China.

The Anglo-Japanese Alliance of 1902 seemed to mark the formal abandonment of Britain's 'isolation'. It also acted as a catalyst to the negotiations for an Anglo-French *entente*, or agreement. The British government became increasingly anxious, in the course of 1903, to reach an agreement with France as tension mounted between Russia and Japan. Lansdowne, the foreign secretary, was alarmed at the prospect that Britain and France might become involved in this conflict (as allies of the main protagonists) if they did not reach an accord. Once the French foreign minister had accepted that Egypt would have to be included in the bargaining, a basis for a colonial understanding existed. In return for a French undertaking not to obstruct British rule in Egypt, Britain accepted France's claim to a predominant influence in Morocco (see page 64). The *Entente Cordiale* of 1904, whilst not constituting an alliance, indicated a mutual desire to put aside past quarrels and co-operate in the future. By 1904, therefore, Britain's international position was much less precarious than it had been in 1897–98. She now had Japan as an ally and France as an *Entente* partner, who might also be able to smooth Britain's path towards an agreement with Russia.

Although not anti-German in intent, the *Entente* had serious implications for Germany. No longer could Berlin count on the antagonism between Britain and France. Holstein's comment that 'no overseas policy is possible against England and France' indicates that *Weltpolitik* had suffered a major setback. Even the 'silver lining' of the Russo-Japanese war turned out to be a false hope. German expectations rose as Russia turned to Berlin for support, but Bülow's hopes of a Russo-German alliance were dashed by the Tsar's insistence on consulting France.

By the end of 1904, therefore, few of the aims of German diplomacy in 1897 had been achieved. Despite the fanfares, *Weltpolitik* had added little to Germany's overseas empire. Admittedly the navy programme was proving very popular in Germany; but the British Admiralty feared in 1904, if not sooner, that 'the German fleet is designed for a possible conflict with Britain'. To meet the challenge, Britain took counter-measures. One consolation for Germany was that Russia's involvement in the Far East made Germany feel more secure in Europe. If the war against Japan weakened Russia's ability to play a major role in European affairs, Germany might be able to alter the European balance of power in her favour. This would make up for some of the disappointments of the period 1897 to 1904.

4 Crises and Tension, 1905–9

KEY ISSUES What were the causes of the crises over Morocco in 1905 and Bosnia in 1908? How close did the Great Powers come to war?

A new and significant factor in the international situation between 1905 and 1909 was the temporary eclipse of Russia as a Great Power.

This major upset in the balance of power was the result of Russia's defeat by Japan in the Far East and the outbreak of revolution at home. Russia's weakness gave Germany an opportunity to free herself from the 'encirclement' which the Franco-Russian Alliance and the Anglo-French *Entente* had seemingly created around her. As we see in the rest of this section, Germany attempted to break the *Entente* by threatening France over Morocco in 1905; and then she tried to weaken the Franco-Russian Alliance by seeking a defensive alliance with Russia. Having failed in both attempts, Germany exploited Russia's continuing weakness by forcing her to climb down in the Bosnian affair in 1909.

a) First Moroccan Crisis

In the spring of 1905, Germany provoked a crisis. The prime object was to inflict a diplomatic defeat on France over the issue of Morocco. In January 1905, a French mission had arrived in Fez, the capital of Morocco, to induce the Sultan to accept a programme of reforms under exclusive French supervision. The French mission had aroused German fears that Morocco would become 'another Tunisia' – another French protectorate. If this happened, German commercial interests would suffer. As a dramatic way of asserting Germany's right to be consulted in such matters, the Kaiser landed at the Moroccan port of Tangier in March 1905. In declaring his intention of upholding the independence of Morocco, the German Emperor was throwing down a challenge to France.

This was made clear in mid-April when the German government demanded an international conference to review the question of Morocco. Germany based this demand on an international agreement signed in 1880, guaranteeing full commercial freedom in Morocco, so she had quite a good case. 'If we allow our feet to be stepped on in Morocco without a protest,' noted a German diplomat, 'we simply encourage others to do the same somewhere else.' Yet if Germany only wanted 'compensation' for French gains in Morocco, she could have used normal diplomatic channels. As it was, her forceful, unorthodox methods caused diplomatic unease.

The French and British governments were puzzled. They could not see the objectives of German policy. It is helpful to regard German policy as operating on two levels. On the surface, they were demanding 'fair shares for all' and the right to be consulted about Morocco's fate. Yet their hidden aim was probably to weaken, if not destroy, the Anglo-French *Entente* (which the German foreign office had described as 'one of the worst defeats for German policy' since the 1894 Franco-Russian Alliance). This was to be achieved by demonstrating that Britain was not a reliable or worthwhile ally. France, it was assumed, would be outvoted at the international conference since other nations would not favour French predominance in Morocco.

Then, humiliated by this check to their aspirations, the French would recognise that co-operation with Germany, not Britain, was essential. To accomplish this, it was necessary to keep up the tension until the French government gave in to Germany's demands. This aggressive policy was pursued through the summer of 1905, backed by the unspoken threat of war. Some historians believe, in fact, that the German Chief of Staff was hoping the crisis would provide an excuse for an attack on France. Certainly Russia's weakness did create a very favourable opportunity for a preventive war against France. But the evidence for this interpretation is not strong.

Germany's actions, coupled with her refusal to negotiate directly with France, created a panic in government circles in Paris. The French army was in no condition to meet a surprise attack, and moreover no help could now be expected from Russia. So the French decided to sacrifice foreign minister Delcassé – the architect of the *Entente Cordiale* – to placate the Germans. His downfall is regarded by some historians as an important motive behind Germany's actions, and it is true that the Kaiser attributed many of the recent setbacks to German diplomacy to Delcassé's skilful mediation between Russia and England. His resignation was regarded as a sign of French weakness in Britain. But at least the British could take heart: if the *Entente* was weakening, it was not needed now to restrain Russia in the Far East, not after Japan's great victory.

In July 1905 the French prime minister gave way to the German demand for a conference that would meet in 1906 at Algeçiras. The 'security and independence' of Morocco would be decided by international agreement, not by Britain and France. Germany had demonstrated that she was a 'World Power' whose views could not be ignored. All that remained to be done was to ensure France's defeat at the conference.

Although the Germans had won their point over Morocco, they failed to capitalise on it. A blow to Germany's hopes of dominating the conference at Algeçiras came with the election of a Liberal government in Britain. The previous foreign secretary, Lansdowne, had judged German policy towards Morocco to be an 'escapade', 'an extraordinarily clumsy bit of diplomacy'. His successor, Sir Edward Grey, was even more critical and so insisted on complete support for France at the conference (even when she rejected reasonable compromises). He even let it be known to the French ambassador, though only as his personal opinion, that Britain would support France if she were attacked by Germany.

After weeks of deadlock at the conference, the Germans finally gave way. She had too few supporters. France secured virtual control of the police and the state bank in Morocco; Germany had to be content with mere guarantees of commercial freedom. Algeçiras was a bad blow for German prestige. As a demonstration of *Weltpolitik*, the Moroccan affair was a disaster. Although France was very vulnerable to pressure in the spring of 1905, Germany had extracted very little advantage from the situation. This was due to a mixture of miscalculation and inconsistency of aims. Direct negotiations with France could have produced positive gains, including 'compensation', if not in Morocco then in the French Congo. The First Moroccan Crisis, therefore, is a good example of the weaknesses of *Weltpolitik* – heavy-handed methods combined with uncertainty of aims.

The outcome was the opposite of what was intended. Far from weakening the Anglo-French *Entente*, the crisis strengthened it. 'Cordial co-operation with France' became a basic principle of British foreign policy under Grey. Furthermore, he authorised 'military conversations' in January 1906 to consider how Britain might aid France if Germany attacked. This has been called a 'revolution in European affairs'. For the first time in 40 years a British government considered despatching an expeditionary force to the Continent. 'The long Bismarckian peace' was over. Several states had contemplated war. It was a sign of things to come.

As a direct result of the first Moroccan Crisis, Grey regarded Germany as a threat to the balance of power in Europe. This was a new anxiety that had not troubled British governments for several decades. The answer to this threat, Grey concluded, was an *entente* that included England, France and Russia so that, 'If it is necessary to check Germany it could then be done'.

b) The Anglo-Russian *Entente*

Negotiations for an agreement with Russia began in April 1906, covering three disputed regions: Persia, Tibet and Afghanistan. Following her defeat in the Far East, Russia was more willing to compromise than in the past. Whereas British ministers had been trying to make an agreement with Russia since at least 1897, many of the Tsar's advisers had not seen much advantage in reducing tension with Britain. The new Russian foreign minister, Izvolsky, however, conscious of Russia's weakness, was anxious to improve her relations with Britain and the other Powers.

After lengthy negotiations from April 1906 to August 1907, agreement was reached on the main issues. Persia was divided into three zones: a Russian zone adjacent to her frontier; a British zone in the south-east covering the Indian border; and a neutral zone separating the two. The agreements on Tibet and Afghanistan also contributed to the security of India, long the key issue in Anglo-Russian antagonism. In effect, both sides agreed not to meddle in the internal affairs of these two 'buffer states'. The Anglo-Russian convention of August 1907 might have begun a new era in Britain's relations with Russia. Yet its significance was for several years uncertain, as the Russians cheated persistently on the Persian agreement.

Grey strove hard to promote good Anglo-Russian relations. This was a sign that Europe, not the empire, was now the focal point of British policy and that Germany, not Russia, was now identified as the main potential enemy. He also tried to take a more tolerant view of Russia's aspirations in the Balkans, recognising that 'good relations with Russia meant that our old policy of closing the Straits' to her warships should end. This willingness to review the issue of the passage of Russian warships between the Black Sea and the Mediterranean made it easier for Izvolsky, the Russian foreign minister, to persuade his colleagues to accept the 1907 agreement.

The strategic and economic importance of the Straits to Russia was steadily increasing in this period. To secure control over 'the keys and gates of the Russian house' was widely regarded as 'Russia's most important task in the 20th century'. So tempting a prize were they that Izvolsky was prepared to give a lot in return for international agreement to changing the Rule of the Straits of 1841, so as to allow Russian warships to pass from the Black Sea to the Mediterranean. In a rather impulsive and dangerous way, Izvolsky launched himself into unofficial talks with other European foreign ministers.

c) The Bosnian Crisis of 1908

The Austro-Hungarian foreign minister, Aehrenthal, was quite receptive to the idea of a 'deal' with Russia since he was considering a project of his own in the Balkans – the annexation of Bosnia. An agreement in 1897 had put the Balkans 'on ice' for a decade. Instead of confrontation, Austria and Russia experimented with co-operation. But now Aehrenthal decided that the time had come to end the ambiguous status of Bosnia which, together with Herzegovina, had been controlled by Austria since the Congress of Berlin in 1878.

Austria's rights in these two provinces seemed in 1908 to be at risk. A new regime, the 'Young Turks' had just come to power in Constantinople, dedicated to the revival of the Ottoman Empire (see page 14). Restoring Bosnia to full Turkish rule was one of their objectives. To prevent this, Austria decided formally to annex the provinces. This would draw a clear line between what was Austrian territory and what was Turkish. The Turks, not surprisingly, saw it differently. To them it looked like seizure of a Turkish province and they demanded compensation. The annexation of Bosnia also angered Serbia because she regarded the Bosnian Serbs as belonging to a future 'Greater Serbia'. There was also the fear that, after Bosnia, she might be the next to be taken over. Too weak to challenge the Austrians by herself, she looked to Russia for support.

Would Russia support Serbia? Izvolsky did not want to. In return for Austria's acceptance of Russia's desire to control the Straits, he agreed in September 1908 – without the knowledge or approval of his prime minister – to the annexation of Bosnia. This was a betrayal of

Serbia, Russia's most recent client state in the Balkans. Russia was in fact in a very embarrassing situation. Tension mounted when Serbia demanded compensation and threatened war. In January 1909 the German government decided that – while Russia was still too weak to face a war – this was a favourable moment for Austria to smash Serbia, so she promised Austria simultaneous mobilisation as a sign of her full support.

Neither France nor Britain showed any such support for Russia. They conveniently blamed Izvolsky for the crisis. Tension continued until late March, when Russia accepted Germany's 'ultimatum' that she recognise the annexation of Bosnia. Serbia, threatened with war by Austria, climbed down and agreed to 'live at peace' with Austria-Hungary.

The Bosnian crisis did not lead to war, but it made Balkan problems worse and created much alarm in Europe. Russia felt humiliated, while Serbia was embittered. It also revealed that the Austro-German Alliance was much more solid than the Triple *Entente*, of Russia, France and Britain. Above all, the crisis ended the Austro-Russian agreement over the Balkans. Further troubles lay ahead.

The years 1905 to 1909 saw a great increase in international tension. Germany's responsibility for this was considerable. She had provoked the Moroccan crisis, exploiting Russia's weakness to threaten France. Although not a prime mover in the opening of the Bosnian affair, she chose to back Austria to the hilt in January 1909, even though her ally had not consulted her about the annexation plan. Germany could have exercised a moderating influence. Instead she chose the opposite path. Before the Bosnian crisis was over, Germany was involved in another source of tension in Europe – the naval race with Britain.

5 Naval Rivalry and the Agadir Crisis, 1908–11

> **KEY ISSUES** Why did these years see an escalation of tension?
> How close did the Great Powers come to war?

a) Overview

In the winter of 1908–9 a 'naval scare' erupted in England through fear of Germany's expanding fleet. Britain had launched in 1906 the new all-big-gun battleship, HMS *Dreadnought*. It had greater firepower and greater speed than anything else afloat. But so superior was it that many experts judged that existing battleships were obsolete – and hence Britain's massive lead in conventional ships no longer seemed to count. There was widespread alarm. By 1908 the damage done to Anglo-German relations made both governments consider proposals to reduce their building programmes, but nothing came of the talks that lasted from 1908 to 1912. British suspicions of Germany deepened further in 1911, when a second crisis arose over Morocco (the Agadir Crisis). Alarmed at how close to war they had been, the British government renewed its efforts for an Anglo-German understanding, but without success.

b) The Naval Race

The prime objective of the Navy Laws of 1898 and 1900, prepared by Admiral von Tirpitz, was to create a powerful battle fleet of about 60 large warships by 1918, designed for operations in the North Sea. The German navy would have grown in size even if Tirpitz had not been appointed chief of the navy office in 1897. Navies were becoming status symbols, and for many Germans naval expansion was a natural expression of their economic power and growing overseas trade. Tirpitz's battle fleet, however, was conceived as a 'power-political instrument' (not as a commerce-protection fleet) to be used as a lever to obtain colonial concessions from Britain. The objective of challenging Britain to secure what he called 'world political freedom' for Germany was implicit in the Tirpitz Plan from the outset. It was not made explicit for obvious reasons, and this made many Britons fear that the Kaiser was in fact preparing for an Anglo-German naval war.

The plan suffered from several miscalculations. The British Admiralty instituted counter-measures from 1902. The re-deployment of ships previously scattered across the globe concentrated a more powerful fleet in home waters and battleship construction was raised to four ships a year from 1905. A major reason for the navy scare of 1908–9 was the drastic reduction in this construction programme by the new Liberal government, elected in 1906, which wanted to reduce expenditure on armaments. The reduction also coincided with an increase in the German building tempo to four a ships a year. Hence the fear that by 1911 Germany could have 13 Dreadnoughts to Britain's 12. Yielding to pressure, the Liberal government reluctantly accepted the demand for no less than eight battleships in the naval estimates for 1909. The naval race was on!

In Britain, opponents of the naval race, including the pro-German members of the Cabinet, pressed for negotiations with Germany to reduce international tension. In Germany, both Bülow and his successor as Chancellor in 1909, Bethmann Hollweg, were alarmed at the strength of British hostility to Germany over the navy issue. But neither Wilhelm II nor Tirpitz was willing to make substantial concessions. For the Kaiser the navy was an obsession – it was 'his fleet' and he angrily rejected any interference with it or with his position as 'Supreme War Lord'.

Negotiations for a naval agreement began in 1909. In reply to Britain's proposals for naval reductions, the Chancellor offered a relaxation of the tempo of construction for three years – but only if

Britain were to agree to remain neutral in a Franco-German or Russo-German war. As Grey commented, such an agreement would leave Britain isolated. Further negotiations in 1910 foundered on the same rock.

The damage done to Anglo-German relations by the naval rivalry was immense. It crystallised, as no other issue could do, all the latent fears and suspicions of Germany's aims. It also caught the attention of the press and public opinion much more forcefully than did other issues. A newspaper editor warned Germany in 1905: 'Any power which challenges Britain's supremacy offers her a menace which she cannot ignore'. In similar vein, the foreign secretary insisted in 1913, 'The Navy is our one and only means of defence and our life depends upon it'.

Germany, by contrast, was first and foremost a continental Power, whose security depended primarily on her army. When the leading military Power became the second naval Power in Europe, Britain's security was felt to be at risk. For the first time for almost half a century, Britons were aware of the danger of invasion. Hence the determination to maintain her naval supremacy regardless of cost. From the German perspective, however, Britain was behaving as though naval supremacy belonged to her by some sort of 'divine right'. But it was dishonest of German leaders, such as Tirpitz and the Kaiser, to pretend that their fleet programme was compatible with Anglo-German friendship. The effect of this naval rivalry in increasing the British government's suspicions of German aims was revealed in 1911.

c) The Agadir Crisis, 1911

The Second Moroccan Crisis began in July 1911 when a German gunboat, the *Panther*, arrived at the Moroccan port of Agadir. The aim was to intimidate the French government into paying substantial territorial compensation in return for recognition of a French protectorate over Morocco. French troops had occupied the capital, Fez, in May, at the Sultan's request, following the outbreak of a revolt. This was widely regarded as prelude to a French take-over. That would break the Algeçiras Act of 1906, and Germany did have a justified grievance.

The crux of the dispute in 1911 was how much territorial compensation Germany could extract from France and what degree of pressure was required to achieve it. There is no doubt that the German foreign minister, Kiderlen, grossly mishandled the situation. He attempted to pull off a 'great stroke' – impressing German public opinion by a prestige victory while at the same time winning French goodwill by accepting a protectorate over Morocco. But he set his target too high – demanding the whole of the French Congo – and conducted German diplomacy in an extremely provocative way. Neither the Chancellor nor the Kaiser shared his enthusiasm for 'thumping the table', as he put it. The French government was prepared to pay what they considered a fair price for Germany's goodwill. But Kiderlen convinced himself that only threats would succeed: 'They must feel that we are prepared to go to the extreme.'

By persisting throughout July in his demand for the whole of the French Congo, Kiderlen made a quick and amicable settlement impossible. His main miscalculation, however, was in not seeing that the unspoken threat to France could only succeed if Britain stayed out of the affair. But the British government, uneasy at the *Panther* incident, became alarmed after their enquiries to Berlin met with total

SOLID.

GERMANY. "DONNERWETTER! IT'S ROCK. I THOUGHT IT WAS GOING TO BE PAPER."

Cartoon from *Punch*, 2 Aug 1911.

silence. In late July, Lloyd George, a powerful Cabinet minister hitherto noted for his pro-German sentiments, gave a speech at the Mansion House in London which demonstrated that Britain had no intention of being ignored in any agreement over Morocco. Once again, the Anglo-French *Entente* was solid (see the cartoon opposite).

After this speech the crisis took a new turn. What had begun as a Franco-German colonial squabble became a major Anglo-German confrontation. The British government was certainly over-reacting when the fleet was put on the alert and plans for British military assistance to France were finalised.

It was a rather bizarre situation. There seemed more likelihood of a war between Britain and Germany than between France and Germany. However, in early November a Franco-German agreement was eventually signed. Germany obtained only two meagre strips of territory in the French Congo – to the fury of German opinion, which had been led to expect a great triumph. Kiderlen's 'great stroke' had failed all round. He had not won popularity for the government and he had antagonised, not conciliated, France. This was an example of *Weltpolitik* at its worst – confusion of aims and heavy-handed methods, resulting in limited gains for Germany at the price of considerable tension.

In England, the risk of war during the Agadir Crisis revived the pressure for Anglo-German conciliation, but the mission of Lord Haldane, the war minister, to Berlin in February 1912 was not a success. The Germans repeated their demand for a neutrality pact, offering in exchange only a slower rate of warship construction.

Having failed to secure a naval limitation treaty with Germany, Britain negotiated a naval agreement with France in 1912–13. In essence, this made Britain responsible for the Channel while France was to guard the Mediterranean. Taken in conjunction with the 'military conversations' revived in 1911, Britain had made an extensive, albeit informal, commitment to the defence of France by 1913. Anglo-Russian naval talks were also held, in secret, in 1914 but no agreement had been reached by the outbreak of war.

d) Conclusion

The period after Bismarck's fall saw a significant escalation of tensions in European affairs. The successors of the 'Iron Chancellor' clearly lacked his diplomatic skill, setting themselves tasks to which they were unequal. That war seemed a possibility during the two Moroccan crisis is testimony to Germany's ineptitude in international affairs. Many people indeed accepted the view that sooner or later there would be war in Europe.

Nevertheless we should not assume that a major war was indeed inevitable. We misuse hindsight if – because we know that war occurred in 1914 – we assume that events were bound to take the course that they did. In addition, we do scant justice to the preceding decades if we see them merely as a build-up to the Great War. France may have signed its alliance with Russia in 1894 and Britain may have been alienated from Germany by the naval race. But, as we shall see, relations between France, Britain and Germany were better in the first six months of 1914 than for many a long year. The First World War would not have come about – certainly not in the way that it did and at the precise time that it did – without the short-term factors, which are addressed in the next chapter.

Summary Diagram
Weltpolitik and European Tensions, 1890–1911

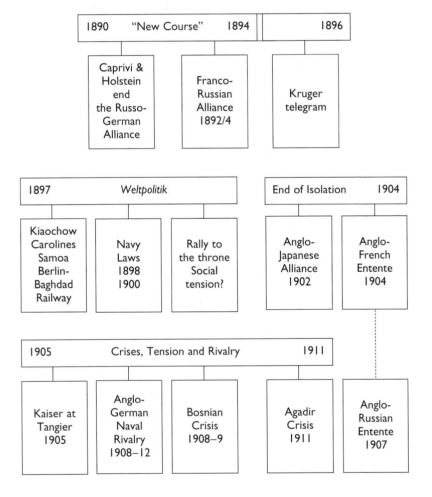

Working on Chapter 4

As you read the chapter, try to identify the ways in which German policy contributed to the growth of international tension. Think particularly about the role of the Kaiser and the explanations of *Weltpolitik*. Which of them seems the more convincing? You should also regard this chapter as providing much of the evidence for the different explanations of the causes of the First World War which you will encounter in the next chapters. Finish your notes by asking how close to a major war the Powers had come in this period.

Answering structured and essay questions on Chapter 4

Many of the questions asked on the period 1890 to 1911 also relate to the causes of the First World War. They will be considered either on pages 109 or 125–6. Questions relating to this chapter focus on the two main issues: the aims and methods of German foreign policy from about 1890 to 1911, and broader aspects of international affairs between these dates.

Answer the following structured question.

a) What motives lay behind the German intervention in Morocco in 1905? (10 marks)
b) What were the results of the 1906 Algeçiras conference? (10 marks)
c) How able was German diplomacy during the 1905–6 Moroccan crisis? (20 marks)

In structured questions, you are often presented with early parts which call for basically factual answers and a final, more analytical part. This is so in the above question, but remember that any consideration of people's motives, as in a), involves matters of judgement. It is also worth pausing over b), remembering that it is often wise to consider short-term and longer-term results. Can the effects of the Algeçiras conference be 'isolated' from the effects of other factors? In answering the final part, you will obviously build on what you have already written. Remember the crucial importance of measuring intentions against effects. You can impress by bringing in evidence of what other states made of Germany's intervention.

The following are typical essay (A2) questions. Remember the importance of dividing up large topics like these into smaller, more manageable questions.

1. Why were relations between Britain and Germany satisfactory in 1890 but unsatisfactory by 1911?
2. 'From the time of Bismarck's fall until 1911, German foreign policy was frequently clumsy and often provocative.' Discuss this verdict.
3. Assess the significance of the Moroccan crises of 1905 and 1911.

These questions relate to German foreign policy itself or to the reaction of other Great Powers to it. Consequently certain key factors could form the basis of an answer to most of them. The factors you choose might include: the aims and methods of *Weltpolitik*; the influence of the Kaiser on German policy; crises and tension; and the nature of the Triple Entente. At this stage it would be useful to make a list of examples of each of the factors given above. Under the heading *Weltpolitik* you would probably include examples such as: overseas expansion; powerful navy; domestic tension; abrasive diplomacy.

Source-based questions on Chapter 4

1 The Climate of Opinion

Read the extracts from Moltke (pp. 71–2), Tolstoy (p. 72) and Steevens (p. 73) and answer the following questions:

a) To what extent was Moltke voicing Social Darwinist ideas? (5 marks)
b) Put into your own words Tolstoy's view of the Russian. Why do you think he was being so critical? (5 marks)
c) What is the significance of the subtitle 'Under the Iron Heel' in the extract from Steevens? (5 marks)
d) Pinpoint the ways in which, according to Steevens, the Frenchman and the German differ. (5 marks)
e) Compare and contrast Steveens' views on the French and the Germans with those of Tolstoy. (10 marks)
f) Using these extracts, and any other information, estimate the extent to which a warlike climate of opinion existed in Europe before 1914. (15 marks)

5 From Balkan Crises to World War, 1912–14

POINTS TO CONSIDER

1912–14 are crucial years, for they culminated in the outbreak of the First World War in August 1914. You need a thorough understanding of the events of this period and of their significance – and of the motives of the key players. Always ask yourself not only what happened but also why. This chapter should be read in conjunction with the next, on the debate between historians on the war's origins.

KEY DATES

1908		Bosnian crisis.
1912		First Balkan War (Balkan League defeats Turkey).
1913		Second Balkan War (Serbia defeats Bulgaria);
	August	Treaty of Bucharest; Austrian ultimatum to Serbia.
1914	28 June	assassination of Franz Ferdinand at Sarajevo in Bosnia;
	5 July	Germany gives the 'blank cheque' to Austria;
	23 July	Serbia receives ultimatum from Austria;
	25 July	Serbia does not accept all Austria's demands;
	28 July	Austria declares war on Serbia;
	30 July	Tsar agrees to general mobilisation;
	1 Aug	Germany declares war on Russia;
	3 Aug	Germany declares war on France;
	4 Aug	Britain declares war on Germany.

The Balkans were the 'powder-keg' of Europe (see page 12). This was a region of chronic instability, due to the decline of Turkish influence, and of Great Power tension. The key issue was that local quarrels here might escalate into a war between Europe's major states. In 1908 there had been a crisis over Bosnia which had threatened to unleash a major war, but Russia and its client state Serbia backed down when confronted by the combined pressure of Austria-Hungary and Germany.

After the conclusion of the Bosnian crisis, the Balkans enjoyed a brief period of relative peace. This ended in 1911 when Italy, in pursuit of her ambitions in Tripoli (modern Libya) – then part of the Ottoman Empire – resorted to naval operations in Turkish waters, including an attack on the Dardanelles.

The revelation of Turkey's weakness in this conflict encouraged the expansionist ambitions of several Balkan states. But the more powerful independent Balkan states became, the more anxious was Austria-Hungary that the south Slavs in her own multi-national empire might seek to join them. Serbia's foreign secretary described

Austria-Hungary around this time as 'not a Fatherland, but rather a prison of numerous nationalities all panting to escape'. Germany had no wish to see her only reliable ally disintegrate, while Russia wished to further her own interests by championing fellow Slavs. Here were explosive ingredients which produced two localised Balkan wars in 1912 and 1913. The following year another Balkan conflict occurred, and the third Balkan war became the First World War.

1 The Balkan Wars, 1912–13

> **KEY ISSUE** Why did conflicts occur in this region, and why were the wars in this period localised affairs?

a) The First Balkan War

In the spring of 1912 Serbia formed a Balkan Alliance with Bulgaria, to which Greece and Montenegro adhered in the autumn. Its main object was to drive Turkey out of the Balkans by freeing Macedonia from Turkish rule and then dividing it amongst themselves. Russian agents with strong Pan-Slavist sympathies played an important part in creating the Balkan League, but they could not control it. The Russians believed that the purpose of the alliance was merely to resist the spread of Austrian influence.

Conrad, the chief of the Austrian general staff, called for the mobilisation of Austria's army when the war began, and the situation for a time looked dangerous. Might the troubles boil over? (See the cartoon on page 97.) After all, Russia might well support its ally Serbia, Germany might well fight if Austria-Hungary did, while the French leader Poincaré insisted that France would join the war if Germany did so. Yet if the Austrian military wanted to join the first Balkan war, the Austrian civilians did not. In particular foreign minister Berchtold urged caution, especially since the Turks might defeat the League. Yet in fact, in two major battles, the Balkan League swiftly defeated the Turkish forces. In December 1912 the Turks sued for peace. Only a local war had taken place.

The war was followed by an international conference in London which included representatives of the belligerent states and the ambassadors of the Great Powers. With both England and Germany playing a mediating role, Grey and the German ambassador were able to induce Russia and Austria-Hungary to give way on some crucial issues and to accept the need for compromises. Thanks to their mediation the most contentious questions were eventually resolved. The Austrians succeeded in their aim of creating an independent Albania (a non-Slav state), but there was acute friction over its boundaries, especially the inclusion of the fortress town of Scutari. Austria was not satisfied, and Russia complained that the concessions she made were not matched by the Austrians.

THE BOILING POINT.

Cartoon from *Punch*, 2 October 1912.

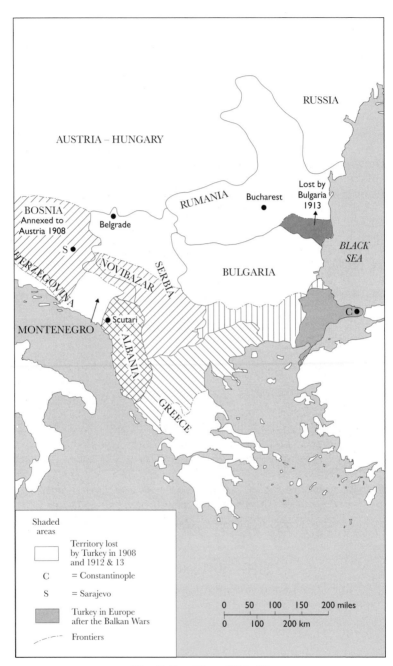

The Balkan Wars, 1912–13.

b) Second Balkan War

The Second Balkan War arose in July 1913 when the victors quarrelled amongst themselves. Serbia had occupied territory which the Bulgarians felt to be rightfully theirs, and Bulgaria now fought against Serbia and Greece. Here was another Balkan war – but would it remain localised or would it escalate into Great Power confrontation? On this occasion Berchtold wanted intervention, and therefore called for German aid, since Serbia might well be supported by Russia. But now the German government called for restraint. After all, the Balkan states were fighting among themselves and might perhaps fight to mutual exhaustion.

Once more a crisis had been isolated. But peace had been preserved partly by a mistaken judgement. Serbia was victorious in the second, as in the first, Balkan war; and, by the Treaty of Bucharest of August 1913, made significant territorial gains. In fact Serbia had doubled in size over the previous two years and could now boast an army of 200,000 men. Military victory for Serbia meant a diplomatic victory for Russia and diplomatic defeat for Austria-Hungary and Germany. Clearly one crisis was over, but the tension had not ended. Indeed it had increased. Austrian politicians felt that, sooner or later, they had to deal with the Serbian menace. Their one consolation was that now the Kaiser had woken up to the realities of Balkan politics. In typically flamboyant manner, Wilhelm II assured his ally, 'I am prepared to draw the sword whenever your moves make it necessary'.

Almost before the second Balkan war had ended, another crisis blew up. Serbian troops were occupying territory which had not been ceded to them by the Treaty of Bucharest. The Serbs had over-reached themselves. Here was the opportunity Berchtold was looking for. He gave the Serbs an ultimatum, to withdraw their troops within one week or face the consequences – and this time he had the backing of the Kaiser and the German government. Russia's reaction was now vital. She had achieved a good deal since the Bosnian crisis in 1908 and could therefore afford to be moderate. Serbian nationalism was an explosive force that could easily involve Russia in a confrontation with Austria, but on this occasion Serbia was advised to comply with the ultimatum and consolidate its position, and the advice was accepted. Europe had advanced to the brink and then backed away. But this was the last crisis to be isolated.

2 The July Crisis, 1914

> **KEY ISSUES** Why did the assassination of Franz Ferdinand have
> such important repercussions? What motivated the policies of
> each country involved?

a) Improved Relations

Against the odds, international affairs improved in the early months
of 1914. This was especially so for Anglo-German relations. The two
former rivals agreed on the building of the Baghdad railway in
Mesopotamia and amicably settled their disagreements over the
future of Portugal's colonies. Furthermore, the naval race was effectively over. In July 1914, as the British sailed away from the Kiel naval
review, a German warship signalled 'Friends in the past, friends for
ever'. 'Since I have been at the Foreign Office,' wrote an official, 'I
have not seen such calm waters.' Sir Edward Grey was of the same
mind, insisting that the 'German government are in a peaceful mood
... and are very anxious to be on good terms with England'.

Franco-German relations were also better than for some time. In
January 1914 the French President dined at the German embassy in
Paris, a social engagement that would not have been accepted in
earlier years, and in the spring a general election produced a left-wing
government of radicals and socialists, pledged to promote peace. It
turned out to be the calm before the storm; but many observers at the
time judged that, if a major war started in the Balkans, it need not
involve either Britain or France.

b) The Assassination

On 28 June 1914, at Sarajevo in Bosnia, the heir to the Austro-
Hungarian throne, Franz Ferdinand, was assassinated by Gavrilo
Princip, a terrorist using weapons supplied by the Serbian terrorist
organisation, the Black Hand. This was the start of a series of events
which, by 4 August, produced war between the Great Powers. These
were fateful weeks for Europe. We know more about them than about
any previous comparable period in the history of mankind. The documentary evidence that survives is voluminous. The sources allow us to
understand *what* happened, and yet there is still great controversy
over *why* events took the course they did.

The motive for the assassination is not altogether clear. The
Archduke Franz Ferdinand may have been chosen at random, as the
victims of terrorists often are. Or the assassins may have chosen him
because of his political views. The Archduke wished to see the south
Slavs achieve self-government within the Habsburg empire, so that
henceforth there would be three 'master races', the Germans, the

Magyars and the south Slavs. This was the sort of compromise disliked by hardline terrorists, who wished the Slavs to quit the empire and join the independent state of Serbia.

Nor can we be completely sure about the complicity of the Serbian government in the assassination. Certainly the assassin had connections with Serbia's Black Hand, of which a colonel in the Serbian General Staff was head. But the assassination was an amateurish affairs. Bombs failed to explode, bullets missed their target, and only the fact that the Archduke's chauffeur failed to stick to the prescribed royal route, and that the car broke out outside a cafe in which Princip was sitting, enabled the murder to succeed.

The Emperor, Franz Joseph, was glad when he heard the news because his nephew had married outside the accepted royal circles. 'God has reasserted the rules.' But his government suspected Serbian involvement in the death and demanded punishment. The Austro-Hungarian foreign minister, Berchtold, told the Emperor that this latest Serbian affront to Austria-Hungary could not be allowed to pass unpunished. In Berchtold's view it was a choice between action or 'renunciation of our Great Power position'. In short, here was the ideal opportunity to act against Serbia.

c) The Key Events

Action against Serbia might well lead Russia to defend her ally, and therefore Berchtold had first to consult Germany. On 5 July the Kaiser, with the approval of his Chancellor, Bethmann Hollweg, gave Austria the so-called 'blank cheque' – unconditional support. Berchtold told the chief of staff, Conrad: 'Germany advises us to strike at once ... Germany will support us unreservedly even if our march into Serbia lets loose a great war.'

If the Austrians had taken swift retaliatory action against Serbia, a European war might have been averted. Although political assassination was nothing new in 1914, many contemporaries, including the Tsar, were shocked by the murder of the heir to the Habsburg throne. Speed and efficiency were not, however, characteristics for which Austria-Hungary was noted. A further impediment to prompt action was the attitude of Count Tisza, the Hungarian prime minister, whose assent was needed to important decisions affecting the Dual Monarchy. He wanted to avoid what he called 'the terrible calamity of a European war' and insisted that, rather than simply attack Serbia, they should instead respond with an ultimatum of demands. This was accepted by the Austrian government, though Berchtold intended that the demands should be so difficult that Serbia would be unable to comply with them. The ultimatum, therefore, was seen as a prelude to war. It was not until mid-July that the demands were ready, and this delay may have been fatal. No longer did Austria seem to be reacting in shock to the death of the heir to its throne.

Berchtold explained his views in these terms on 21 July:

1 It was increasingly certain that the subversive activity pursued on
   Bosnian soil ... and with ramifications in Dalmatia, Croatia, Slavonia and
   Hungary could be checked only by energetic action at Belgrade [Serbia's
   capital], where the threads run together; and that a new grouping of
5 Powers is coming into being in the Balkans with the connivance of
   Rumania and Russia, with the destruction of the Monarchy as its ultimate aim ... In drafting the note to Serbia it seemed to us essential, not
   only to document before the whole world our good right to put certain demands to Serbia for the preservation of our internal tranquillity;
10 but to formulate these demands in such a way as would oblige Serbia to
   take up a clear position against propaganda hostile to the Monarchy, as
   regards the past and in the future, and as would give us a chance of
   making our voice heard in the matter in future. For us it was not a question of humiliating Serbia, but of bringing about a clear situation regard-
15 ing Serbia's relations with the Monarchy as a neighbour, and, as a
   practical result, either, in the event of our demands being accepted, a
   thorough clearing up of the situation in Serbia with our co-operation
   or, in the event of their being refused, settling the matter by force of
   arms and paralysing Serbia as much as possible.

Delivery of the ultimatum to Belgrade was further delayed until the
end of the French President's visit to Russia on 23 July, in case his
presence in St Petersburg facilitated Franco-Russian solidarity. The
ultimatum gave the Serbian government 48 hours to reply to the following terms:

1 The Royal Serbian Government will pledge itself to the following:
   1. to suppress every publication likely to inspire hatred and contempt
   against the Monarchy or whose general tendencies are directed against
   the integrity of the latter;
5 2. to begin immediately dissolving the society called the *Narodna
   odbrana* (Black Hand); to seize all its means of propaganda and to act in
   the same way against all the societies and associations in Serbia, which
   are busy with the propaganda against Austria-Hungary;
   3. to eliminate without delay from public instruction everything that
10 serves or might serve the propaganda against Austria-Hungary, both
   where teachers or books are concerned;
   4. to remove from military service and from the administration all offi-
   cers and officials who are guilty of having taken part in the propaganda
   against Austria-Hungary, whose names and the proofs of whose guilt
15 the Imperial Government will communicate to the Royal Government;
   5. to consent that Imperial Officials assist in Serbia in the suppressing of
   the subversive movement directed against the territorial integrity of the
   Monarchy.

The Austrian ultimatum shocked several foreign ministers by its sever-
ity, but the cleverly worded Serbian reply led many, including the
Kaiser, to regard it as conciliatory. The real attitude of the Serbian

government, however, was obscure since, while the reply actually rejected very little, it did not clearly accept very much of the ultimatum. Two factors seem to have influenced the decision not to accept the Note unequivocally. The first was fear that the degree of complicity of the Serbian government would be revealed. The second was the assurances of support received from St Petersburg on 25 July. From this moment on there was little chance of the conflict being limited to Austria-Hungary and Serbia.

d) Reactions of the Powers

i) Germany

The Kaiser's reaction to the Sarajevo murder had been to insist that the Serbs be dealt with once and for all. Hence he gave the 'blank cheque' on 5 July, urging Austria to act immediately. But the Kaiser did not necessarily believe that a major war would ensue. After all, Russia might stay out if Austria seemed to be avenging the death of the heir to the throne. For this reason the Germans urged speedy Austrian action. In early July the German leaders thought that swift retaliatory action against the Serbs was necessary. As late as 18 July, the German foreign minister maintained: 'The more boldness Austria displays and the more strongly we support her, the more likely Russia is to keep quiet'. Bethmann Hollweg summed up German policy on 14 July by calling it a 'leap in the dark'. Clearly Germany was risking involvement in a major war. Why was it worth taking the risk?

There were probably several reasons. First, failure to act would undermine Austria-Hungary's credibility as a Great Power and reduce her value to Germany as an ally. Second, many Germans felt that they were being encircled by the Triple Entente and that, as each year passed, Germany would be less likely to defeat her enemies. German feelings of vulnerability were summed up by a headline from 1913 in the newspaper *Der Tag*: 'Enemies all round – permanent danger of war from all sides'. In particular, it was well known that Russia was implementing important improvements to her armed forces. Russia began the Great Military Programme in 1914. Her speed of mobilisation was due to increase to a mere 18 days by 1917, and if this happened the Schlieffen Plan (see page 75), which was based on the idea that Germany would have six weeks in which to defeat France, would be fatally undermined. According to Bethmann Hollweg, 'the future lies with Russia, she grows and grows, and lies on us like a nightmare'. Hence Moltke, the German Chief of Staff, believed in July 1914 that 'a moment so favourable from a military point of view might never occur again'. Third, a major war might well solve Germany's domestic political problems.

Weltpolitik and the building of a great navy had not transformed the Kaiser into a popular hero. Quite the contrary. The construction of the navy had proved very expensive, as had the increases in the size of the German army signalled by the Army bills of 1912 and 1913. By 1914 the socialists (SPD) were the largest single party in the Reichstag, with 110 seats, and in fact so unpopular was the government that none of its measures could command a majority of votes. Hence government was being carried on by emergency decree. One way out of this deadlock might be a major war, which would rally the people behind the Kaiser. Norman Stone has asked the pertinent question: 'Would Bethmann Hollweg have to conquer Europe in order to rule Germany?'

But perhaps it would not come to war. Having escalated the crisis, Berlin showed signs of having second thoughts. After giving the 'blank cheque', the Kaiser went off on a three-week cruise; and when he returned home, and saw Serbia's reply to the ultimatum, he decided that there was no longer any cause for war. By this time, however, events were beginning to move too fast for statesmen to control. The Kaiser called for negotiations, but the Austrians replied that it was too late. Vienna took heart from a telegram on 28 July from Moltke, urging them to war. Berchtold commented wryly: 'What a laugh – who rules in Berlin!' Almost immediately, Austria declared war on Serbia, whose capital, Belgrade, was soon bombarded by Austrian gunboats on the river Danube, even though the Austro-Hungarian army was not ready for action against Serbia for another two weeks. A war – albeit only a local war at this stage – had begun

From then onwards, the Germans seemed set on major war. But it had to be a conflict which would rally all the German people, including the socialists. Hence the Fatherland had to be seen to be in danger: therefore Germany could not make the first aggressive move. News of Russian mobilisation was therefore highly welcome to the German cabinet. Admiral von Muller wrote in his diary on 1 August: 'The mood is brilliant. The government has managed magnificently to make us appear the attacked party.' Emotion was intense in Germany at this time. Even the usually level-headed General von Falkenhayn insisted that 'Even if everything turns out disastrously, it will have been worth it.' War was certainly popular. Germany's internal problems were forgotten as a welter of nationalistic fervour gripped almost the whole nation.

ii) Russia

The Russian foreign minister was shocked by the terms of the Austrian ultimatum to Serbia on 24 July. 'This means a European war', Sazonov exclaimed. He interpreted Austria-Hungary's action as a deliberate provocation. Perhaps he might have reacted differently had he believed that Serbia had been involved in the assassination.

Important decisions on which Russian policy was based for the remainder of the crisis were taken on 24–25 July. At the meeting of the Council of Ministers, Sazonov argued that Russia's conciliatory stance in earlier Balkan disputes had been interpreted by Germany as a sign of weakness. Russia's prestige with the Slav nations, as well as her influence in the Balkans, was at stake. In addition, German arrogance towards the Slavs was an affront to the dignity of Russia, the leading Slav state. In this crisis, therefore, Russia must stand firm – even at the risk of war. Within a matter of days Russia decided to mobilise her army. There was little agreement about whether there should be partial or general mobilisation. The Tsar was in favour of the former, but in the end his general staff convinced him to accept general mobilisation, orders for which went out on 30 July. Even so, the Tsar, Nicholas II, telegraphed to his cousin, Wilhelm II, that his army would take no provocative action.

The Russian government was clearly prepared to fight (against the advice of some of the Tsar's counsellors, including Rasputin). Public opinion, as expressed in the press and the parliament, was in favour of supporting Serbia, even at the cost of war. On the other hand, it seems very unlikely that the Russians positively desired a major war. Mobilisation for them meant preparation for a possible war. The Germans, however, interpreted mobilisation as the virtual equivalent to a declaration of war, and Germany's Schlieffen Plan meant that the German army would have to attack and defeat France before moving eastwards to combat Russian forces.

The modifications Moltke made to the original Schlieffen plan only increased the importance of speed, especially in the first few days of the war. For example, the Belgian fortress of Liège had to be seized on day 3 of mobilisation – a crucial fact kept secret from both the Chancellor and the Kaiser. Hence, whereas other European governments could honestly echo the French claim that 'Mobilisation is not war', Germany could not. Russia's mobilisation was therefore followed by Germany's mobilisation accompanied by a declaration of war on 1 August.

iii) France and Britain

The problem with Germany's plans was that France had not yet decided to join the war. How would they react? Between 22 and 28 July the French President and prime minister were at sea, returning from Russia, and hence out of contact with the government. The French ambassador at St Petersburg assured the Russian government emphatically that it could rely on French aid against Germany. Poincaré, the President, also believed that war was inevitable. But, bearing in mind the lesson of 1870 (see page 2), he was determined that France should take no provocative action and should not be seen as the aggressor. In addition, the French government of the day was far less warlike than he. In the end, France's reaction did not really matter. Russian mobilisation took place without their knowledge, and on 3 August – before the French had decided what to do – Germany declared war on France. The Germans protested that French aeroplanes had bombarded Nuremberg. It was a blatant lie. The truth of the matter was that Germany could not wait: the Schlieffen Plan had to be implemented without delay.

The British foreign secretary, Sir Edward Grey, has been criticised for not making clear that Britain would support France if she were attacked by Germany. In fact, he had no authority to make such a statement. Critics have also complained that he had aligned Britain too closely with France, and yet the terms of the *Entente Cordiale* left Britain freedom of manoeuvre in the July Crisis. Grey himself wanted Britain to fight against Germany, but the British cabinet and the House of Commons were divided on the issue. What resolved matters was Germany's violation of Belgian neutrality on 3 August. Britain had guaranteed this neutrality in a treaty of 1839. Demonstrations took place in Trafalgar Square and crowds assembled outside Buckingham Palace shouting 'We want war!' Britain declared war on Germany the following day, 4 August. The issue of Belgian neutrality unleashed powerful anti-German forces in Britain, though the deeper reason for Britain's participation in the war was given by *The Times* on 6 August: intervention was 'not merely a duty of friendship. It is ... an elementary duty of self-preservation ... We cannot stand alone in a Europe dominated by any single power'.

3 Conclusion

> **KEY ISSUE** What are some of the most important questions to ask about the start of the Great War?

The war that started in 1914 was a third Balkan war (between Serbia, Austria-Hungary and Russia); but it was also another, more fearsome war, which contemporaries called the Great War. Its causes encompass the complex and combustive situation in the Balkans, a situation that produced three wars in as many years. It is not difficult to appreciate why the Balkan region was so dangerous or why another conflict started there in 1914. More difficult to decide is why all of Europe's Great Powers became involved.

'Once the dice were set rolling,' said Bethmann Hollweg, 'nothing could stop them.' But when did the dice start rolling – when should we begin a study of the origins of the First World War? Clearly the causes can be traced a long way back into the past – to the Agadir crisis of 1911, or the first Moroccan crisis of 1905, or even to the unification of Germany in 1871. Just how important were the long-term, as against the short-term, factors?

According to Princip, in an Austrian jail, 'If it hasn't been me, they would have found some other excuse.' Perhaps the assassination on

28 June 1914 was just the 'occasion' of war, determining the timing of something which was bound to happen anyway. Yet international affairs had undoubtedly been improving in 1914. Who is to say that this trend might not have carried on if Princip has not done the deed?

Historians argue about the relative importance of short- and long-term factors in producing the war. But clearly we have to take account of both.

As for the responsibility of the participant countries, we should say that all of them had been responsible, to varying degrees, in producing the tension and crises that preceded the war. It is also true that many 'statesmen' entered the war with a willingness that has shocked later generations. Many of them believed, foolishly, that it would be 'all over by Christmas'. But not all countries bear the same degree of responsibility for the actual outbreak of war. Certainly Britain cannot be allowed to bear much blame, for the war was under way by the time she joined. Similarly, France was victim not aggressor, and she had no choice but to defend herself. Austria-Hungary undoubtedly wanted a war, though if possible just a war against Serbia: and her share of responsibility is significant because of this. But she could not start a world war – she was too weak for that.

Russia's role was undoubtedly significant. Without her support Serbia would not have pursued such expansionist policies in the Balkans. And if Russia had not mobilised her forces, there would have been no Great War. Yet it is hard to find any positive wish for war on her part in the surviving evidence. She ended up in a war which she was prepared to fight but which she had no wish to fight.

What of Germany? Clearly her role was of great importance. She urged Austria on, with the 'blank cheque', and it was she who declared war on Russia on 1 August. Furthermore, she violated Belgian neutrality and invaded France, thus bringing Britain into the conflict. There is some evidence that the German government had wanted to keep Britain out of the war, but clearly the Germans took the initiative in escalating the conflict. It is hard to avoid the conclusion that the main responsibility for the actual outbreak of war in 1914 (as distinct from the larger issue of war origins) seems to lie with Germany. It is also difficult to find a single constructive move that Germany made throughout the July Crisis. Did she act the way she did out of design? Or did Germany blunder into war? For an understanding of this key issue we need to study the interpretations which historians have put forward over the years – and this forms the substance of the next chapter.

Study Diagram
From Balkan Crises to World War, 1912–14

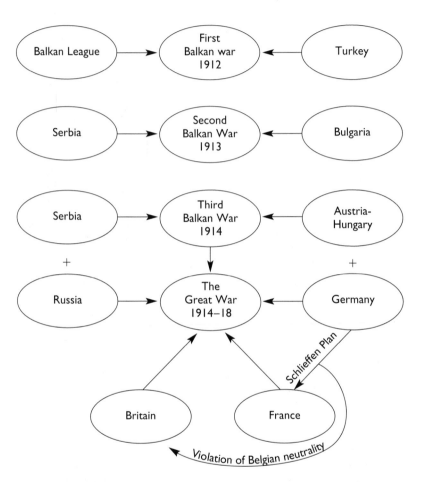

It is essential to compile a good narrative of events from the material in this chapter. Do not be put off if you find that the sequence at first seems very complicated. (Imagine how people at the time felt!) Only if you are confident of *what* happened can you begin to understand *why*. In your notes on the final section, the Conclusion, you can begin to grapple with plausible explanations for what occurred. Remember that any theory about the origins of the war must be measured against the hard facts contained in the chronology. But do not make up your mind yet. First read the next chapter.

Answering structured questions on Chapter 5

Examples of essay questions will be provided at the end of the next chapter. In the meantime, attempt the following structured question:

a) Why did the first Balkan War take place in 1912? (5 marks)
b) Why did a further war occur in the Balkans in 1913? (5 marks)
c) Why did the Great Powers remain neutral in both these conflicts? (10 marks)

This question should test your knowledge of the events of this period. Do not forget to devote most time to the third part. Here you have to exercise your judgement. Do not forget to mention Austria's ultimatum to Serbia after the treaty of Bucharest. Hence you have to explain not only why Austria and Germany remained passive during the Balkan Wars but why Russia urged restraint on Serbia.

Source-based questions on Chapter 5

1 The July Crisis, 1914
Read carefully the extracts from Berchtold and from the Ultimatum to Serbia, given on page 102. Answer the following questions:

a) What was 'the Monarchy' referred to by Berchtold? (3 marks)
b) Why did 'the Monarchy' regard Serbia as a threat to its survival? (7 marks)
c) Which of the demands made in the Ultimatum put into effect Berchtold's insistence that Serbia should 'give us a chance of making our voice heard in the matter in the future' (line 13)? (5 marks)
e) How far is it justifiable to claim that Serbia could only have accepted the Ultimatum if she had been prepared to surrender her independence? (5 marks)
f) How convincing is Berchtold's claim that 'for us it was not a question of humiliating Serbia' (line 17) Use evidence from both extracts in your answer. (10 marks)
g) Use these documents, and other information, to explain what share of responsibility Austria-Hungary must bear for the outbreak of the First World War. (20 marks)

6 Conclusion: The Origins of the First World War

POINTS TO CONSIDER

After reading the previous chapter, you should have a good knowledge of what happened from June to August 1914. You should also have formed preliminary ideas about why certain key players acted in the way they did. This chapter builds upon this knowledge by introducing you to the 'historiographical' debate, i.e. the debate between historians, about what caused the war and who was responsible. It is important to realise that not all views are mutually exclusive: some simply look at what happened from different perspectives. But others are contradictory, and you have to choose between them.

1 Introduction

> **KEY ISSUE** What are the difficulties associated with any explanation of the First World War?

The First World War was a cataclysm for Europe. So high was the total of deaths during the conflict that almost every European family suffered loss. No wonder that the causes of the war have been hotly debated from 1914 to the present day. Yet it would probably take a lifetime to read all the books and articles that have been written explaining why the war began, and several lifetimes to digest all the documentary sources hidden away in a dozen archives. In many ways the whole topic has become unmanageable. We have to deal with a large time-span, since no one knows when the origins of the war really began. We have to deal with a large geographical area, since we must study all the countries who entered the war. In addition, we cannot confine ourselves simply to diplomatic sources, since the 'real' causes of the war may lie in economic rivalries or the realm of ideas. What follows can therefore be no more than an introduction.

Here are some initial ideas that may prove useful:

- Historians' views on the causes of the war tend to vary between two poles. At one extreme is the notion that 'Germany willed the war'; at the other is the idea that 'The nations of Europe stumbled into war.' Between these two extremes is a broad central position that holds that while no one nation can be held entirely responsible for the war, some nations were more responsible than others.
- It is also useful to distinguish between the tensions that preceded the war and the actual outbreak of hostilities. The countries most responsible for the former may not be those most to blame for the latter.

- It is also useful to distinguish between 'man-made forces' (such as expansionist ambitions, war plans and so on) and 'impersonal forces' (such as capitalism or imperialism). The limitation of impersonal forces is that, though they may explain why a war was likely, they fail to explain why a particular war broke out at a precise time. They need therefore to be linked in some way with the man-made forces that do show how a diplomatic crisis became a European war.
- James Joll's uses the phrase 'patterns of concentric circles', by which he links the 'impersonal forces' to the July crisis (see the diagram on page 124). The causes of the war form a complex pattern, interacting with each other. We need to see the outbreak of war in terms of decisions taken by political leaders, set against the background of impersonal factors, which may well have limited the options open to them.

2 Germany and the Debate on War Origins

> **KEY ISSUES** What are the main interpretations explaining why the war started? How important are the ideas of Fritz Fischer?

a) German War Guilt?

There has been little agreement as to who or what caused the First World War. Hence the student is confronted by a bewildering variety of interpretations. One reason for this is that each generation of historians looks at the problem from a different point in time; another is that they have different national perspectives; and a third reason is that they sometimes find new evidence. A fourth is that the facts do not 'speak for themselves': they have to be interpreted by human – often all too human – historians.

Over the years attention has tended to focus on Germany's responsibility, a highly controversial area. After the war, the victors had little doubt that Germany, and to some extent her allies, had been to blame. In article 231 (the famous 'war guilt clause) of the Treaty of Versailles, it was stated that Germany and her allies had deliberately started the war. (In the British general election at the end of the war, there were calls to 'Make Germany Pay' and 'Hang the Kaiser'. Articles in the press debated whether Wilhelm II should be boiled in oil or merely hanged, drawn and quartered.) For a time, this remained a 'consensus' view, at least outside Germany and Austria.

Yet the Germans did not believe that had been guilty of starting the war. German historians published large volumes of documents to show that they had not been at fault, and gradually most historians were won over. In the first volume of his war memoirs, published in 1923, Winston Churchill wrote that 'One rises from the study of the causes of the Great War with a prevailing sense of the defective control of individuals upon world fortunes.' A few years later Lloyd

George, who had helped to write the Treaty of Versailles, insisted that no one had been to blame: 'the nations slithered over the brink into the seething cauldron of war'. Events simply got out of hand. Bethmann Hollweg, Germany's Chancellor in 1914, was often quoted: 'Once the dice were set rolling, nothing could stop them'. The war had been an accident, and yet at the same time there was something inevitable about it. 'Great armament', said Grey, foreign secretary when war started, led 'inevitably to war'.

For a long time this was easily the most popular explanation. The war had been caused by misunderstandings and miscalculations. This view was flourishing in the 1950s, when a Franco-German conference of historians concluded that 'the documents do not allow one to ascribe to any one government or people in 1914 the conscious desire for a European war'. It was a very desirable verdict at a time when France and Germany were, in 1957, signing the Treaty of Rome, which started the European Community. Clearly the origins of the war were not of solely academic interest: they had a political dimension. This was live, not dead, history.

Fritz Fischer found this in the 1960s. With Fischer we come full circle, returning to notions of German war guilt. His writings aroused enormous emotional hostility in Germany. He was called 'a national masochist' and 'intellectual flagellant'. There were calls for him to resign his university professorship, and the West German government attempted to stop him giving a lecture tour in the United States.

b) The Fischer Thesis

Fischer's starting point was a document he discovered, the September Memorandum, a statement of war aims written by Bethmann Hollweg and dated 9 September 1914 and calling for a German-dominated *Mitteleuropa* (Middle Europe), as well as colonial acquisitions in Africa. This statement was so detailed that Fischer thought it could not have been merely improvised at the start of the war. These ideas must, he suspected, have been formulated earlier, during the July Crisis itself. Perhaps indeed the German government had gone to war to achieve these aims?

Subsequent research confirmed his suspicions. There was no drift to war – there was a 'drive to war' and Germany was 'grasping at world power'. The army bills of 1912 and 1913 were, he decided, designed to equip Germany for a major war. Even more important to Fischer was a record he discovered of a top-level meeting at the Royal Palace in Berlin on Sunday 8 December 1912. At this meeting the Kaiser looked to the future: he said that Austria would at some point have to 'deal energetically' with Serbia, and that if Russia supported Serbia, 'which she evidently would', Germany would have to get involved. A large-scale war would take place, in which France would be bound to support Russia. Tirpitz then said that the navy would not be ready for another 18 months, while Moltke judged that, if war were delayed for longer than 18 months, the balance of military power would shift in favour of Russia.

Add on 18 months to December 1912, and of course you get the summer of 1914. This was no coincidence, according to Fischer. The German government wanted a war, planned for war and got the war it wanted. The 'blank cheque' of 5 July was the Kaiser's way of ensuring that the crisis escalated. Admittedly the Kaiser got cold feet when he saw Serbia's response to the ultimatum, and Moltke had to step in to ensure that war did take place; but this last-minute failure of nerve should not disguise Germany's war guilt. Germany declared war on Russia on 1 August on hearing of her mobilisation, but this was merely an excuse to start a war. She desired war to achieve territorial gains and also to solve the constitutional deadlock whereby the German government could not achieve a majority in the Reichstag.

c) Fischer and his Critics

Fischer's interpretation has several virtues. It is based on solid evidence and it is clear-cut and simple. It makes sense of pre-war tensions and of the outbreak of war, seeing them as part of a single process. But to his critics, Fischer's views do not take account of all the evidence and are far too simple.

Several historians have attacked the centrepiece of Fischer's thesis, the weight he gives to the September Memorandum. It has been said that it was a response to the series of early German victories at the start of the war: Germany's war aims in September had escalated since the declarations of war the previous month. The Memorandum has also been seen as an attempt by Bethmann Hollweg to secure his own position as Chancellor: many critics thought him weak, and so he tried to steal their thunder by calling for extensive annexations. Either way, the document sheds no light whatsoever on why Germany went to war. Many have also found Fischer's depiction of Bethmann Hollweg as a ruthless expansionist quite unconvincing. Nor do critics believe that the erratic Kaiser was capable of sticking to a plan for 18 months. And if he did expect a major war to erupt, why did he go off on a three-week cruise after issuing the 'blank cheque'? Bethmann Hollweg said on 7 July that 'our support for Austria can lead to world war' – *can* not *will* or *must*. Hence many historians believe that Germany's war guilt lay in risking a major war not in deliberately starting one.

It has been said that Fischer, having misunderstood the September Memorandum, then interpreted events to fit in with his preconceived view of German war guilt. In short, he misused hindsight. This led him to focus only on those elements of the complex story which suited him. He also failed to see Germany's actions in a proper international context. For instance, Fischer insisted that the army bills of

1912 and 1913 were the start of a 'drive to war' – but he failed to see increases in the Germany army alongside those of other Powers.

In 1912 the German army increased by 29,000 men to a total of 650,000. Her ally, Austria-Hungary, had 450,000 troops. Yet Russia had an army of 1,300,000 and France of 600,000 men. Germany was still relatively vulnerable. The following year, 1913, Germany decided to increase her army by well over 100,000 men so that, by 1914, German forces would total almost 800,000 men. Yet this was not necessarily an aggressive move, since in July 1913 the French decided to increase their period of military service from two to three years. The French army would soon be equal with, if not superior to, the German.

The 'Fischer thesis' – that Germany willed the war in 1914 – has had an enormous impact on historical opinion. It reopened an issue which had fallen into a stale consensus. Yet many historians do not accept its exclusive emphasis on Germany's responsibility or the motives alleged for it. The real issue in 1914, they believe, was not a bid for world domination or an attempt to solve domestic political problems but the desperate need to preserve Austria-Hungary's position as a Great Power and ally. Their charge against Germany is that she pursued in an aggressive way what was an essentially defensive aim. In particular, she did not make a single constructive move in July to defuse the crisis; instead she took a number of calculated risks, 'a series of gambles that did not work out'.

The Fischer 'school' have created a distorted picture of the diplomatic situation in July 1914 which needs to be corrected by a proper Europe-wide perspective – in short, by examining policy-making in other European capitals during the crisis.

3 The Responsibility of Other Powers

> **KEY ISSUE** What degree of responsibility for the war should be assigned to Russia, Austria-Hungary, France and Britain?

No longer do historians look almost exclusively at Germany's responsibility for the war. Many recent books have focused on why the other Powers entered the war.

a) Austria-Hungary

Although there is no doubt that Austria-Hungary was under pressure from Germany to retaliate against Serbia in July 1914, there is much evidence to suggest that she needed no prompting from Berlin to respond to the Sarajevo incident.

The assassination of 28 June 1914 presented Austria-Hungary with a basic dilemma. Inaction meant 'the renunciation of our Great

Power position', as the foreign minister put it. Action against Serbia, however, would might well result in war with Russia. The stark choice seemed to be between the decline and disintegration of the empire and the risk of defeat in war. With German support, however, the chances of defeat would be greatly reduced. Yet some historians have argued that even without the 'blank cheque', Austria might have gone to war, risking the dangers of Russian retaliation, so great was the threat from Serbia perceived to be.

Austrian responsibility for the outbreak of war may be all the greater because of her delay in responding to Franz Ferdinand's death. Had the Austrians delivered a rapid punitive strike against the Serbian capital, Belgrade, the outcome could well have been quite different. But, as the German Chancellor complained, 'They seem to need an eternity to mobilise'. The German government constantly pressed their ally to act quickly, largely in the hope that prompt action would permit the conflict to be kept localised. But the ultimatum to Serbia was not delivered until almost a month after Sarajevo. On the other hand, she then may have acted too quickly. The ultimatum had a time limit of only 48 hours, and within three days of the response Austria had declared war on Serbia. Hence there was no time for mediation. Furthermore, the Austrian government ignored the Kaiser's suggestion on 28 July to halt military operations.

On a number of counts, therefore, Austria-Hungary contributed to the escalation of a major diplomatic crisis into a European war. This conclusion is only of significance, of course, if we reject Fischer's view that Germany was intent on a general war from the outset. If he is right, then what the Austrians did in the course of the crisis is obviously of much less importance.

b) Russia

Russia's responsibility for the outbreak of war in 1914 stems from her policy in the Balkans before 1914 and the decisions she took during the July Crisis itself. Several historians regard Russian policy as quite provocative. In the first place it seems clear that Russia, not Austria-Hungary, was the expansionist force in the Balkans. The Balkan Wars can even be regarded as Russia's wars fought 'by proxy' (through the Balkan League). Secondly, she was unable – or perhaps unwilling – to restrain or control the explosive force of Slav nationalism. Russia's promise of support to Serbia must have influenced her decision not to accept the ultimatum; and, in late July 1914, Russia was the first of the Great Powers to mobilise. Admittedly Russia's prestige as a Balkan Power and as a protector of the Slavs was at stake – but her survival was not, unlike the case of Austria-Hungary.

c) France and Britain

Most historians do not regard these two Powers as playing a crucial role in the outbreak of war (see page 105). In 1912, France appears to have given a sort of 'blank cheque' to Russia by promising French support under any circumstances. This pledge was renewed in 1914, but this time it seems to have been the work of her ambassador in St Petersburg rather than official policy from Paris. The British government had no positive desire for war in 1914, though perhaps she might have done more to try to restrain Russia. The responsibility of France and Britain lies not so much in the July Crisis itself as in the preceding years, when tensions were building up. Might they have done more to promote better relations between the Great Powers, especially between themselves and Germany?

4 The Balkans

> **KEY ISSUE** How important were Balkan issues in producing war?

Balkan problems have naturally long been regarded as a major factor in the origins of the First World War. But did the situation in the Balkans cause, or merely occasion, the war in 1914?

If Fischer is correct in asserting that Germany wanted to launch a war around the summer of 1914, then the Sarajevo murder simply provided her with the excuse that she wanted. On the other hand, those historians who do not accept Fischer's thesis regard Balkan problems as playing a more important part in the origins of the war.

In the early 20th century, the crucial issue in the Balkans was the conflict between Austria-Hungary and Serbia. Serbian nationalism, an expansive force seeking to unite all Serbs into a Greater Serbia, was a deadly threat to the multinational Habsburg empire. Serbia's sense of grievance at the Austrian annexation of Bosnia, which had a large Serb population, was matched by Austrian alarm at Serbia's territorial expansion as a result of the Balkan Wars. Added to this dangerous brew was Russian support for the Serbs. Two of the Great Powers were now involved with the fate of one of the Balkan states. To make matters worse, Russia was unable to control Serbia, and the Serbian government was unable fully to control nationalistic secret societies and the army. These were the ingredients which produced a 'Third Balkan War' in 1914.

5 Ideas, Domestic Politics and Military Plans

> **KEY ISSUE** How important in causing the war were these three factors?

One fruitful way of considering the origins of the war it to focus not on particular countries but on issues which affected several countries. One of these is the climate of opinion – the idea that war was natural or even inevitable and moreover a glorious adventure, and that one's enemies were members of lesser nations and therefore likely to be all the more easily defeated (see pages 70–74). Such assumptions did not, of course, automatically translate themselves into deeds. Yet we might expect politicians to be influenced by public opinion to some extent and also themselves to share popular assumptions. There is certainly evidence that many decision-makers accepted war, or at least were prepared to risk war, without any moral qualms. The Hungarian premier Tisza was aware of the horrors of war and so was Britain's Sir Edward Grey – who commented at the start of war that 'The lamps are going out all over Europe; we shall not see them lit again in our life-time' – but these were exceptions. Surely the unrealistic image of war that had been propagated in the previous generation must have made politicians the more willing to indulge in it.

There is also plentiful evidence that large sections of European society welcomed war in 1914. According to Adolf Hitler, 'The struggle of the year 1914 was not forced on the masses – no, by the living God – it was desired by the whole people.' This may be an unbalanced generalisation; but while not everyone desired war, many people did.

Public opinion may provide another clue. Politicians may have provoked war knowing that it would be popular and that this popularity would solve their domestic problems. In Britain, for instance, war had a unifying effect. The suffragettes suddenly became loyal supporters of the Liberal government, which they had previously attacked; and the warring factions in Ireland vied with each other in their patriotism. French society was also unified, and so was that in Germany, where the constitutional deadlock was immediately overcome. These were the effects of joining the war – may they have been the *intended* effects? Did governments go to war to solve their domestic problems? It would be surprising if politicians had not given at least some consideration to the likely domestic effects of going to war.

Or perhaps the real causes of war are located in the military plans of the generals? Certainly the Schlieffen plan was remarkably important in 1914. It specified that Germany had to fight France before Russia, and this meant that France had to enter the war whether she wanted to or not. Similarly the Russians had planned for general mobilisation, and when the Tsar wanted partial mobilisation he was told that it was 'technically impossible'. Several historians believe that there came a stage when the general took over from the politicians – on 28 July in Germany, when Moltke brushed aside the Kaiser's doubts and urged Vienna to declare war on Serbia – and then the inflexible military plans took over from the generals.

In all countries there was a glorious and unrealistic image of war, in all countries there were domestic problems which war might overcome, and in all countries there were inflexible military plans. These constitute important elements of the origins of the First World War. But they do not 'solve' the issue of responsibility for the war. We still have the problem of examining how far these factors influenced the actions of particular countries.

6 Alliances, International Anarchy and Armaments

> **KEY ISSUE** How important was the division of Europe into two 'armed camps'?

The alliance system is often seen as an important factor in the breakdown of peace, part of the 'pattern of concentric circles' of causal factors that limited the options available to statesmen in the July Crisis. But how important was it?

At first sight the alliances seem of fundamental importance in 1914. They may not explain the causes of antagonism, but they surely show why the crisis that erupted in the Balkans in June 1914 was not isolated. Was it not the alliance system that dictated that Germany should support Austria-Hungary and France support Russia? A note of caution must be introduced, however. First, we should note that the alliance system had kept the peace for a long time. The linking of two Powers had often meant that one of them restrained the other, as Bismarck had intended when, for instance, he signed the Austro-German Alliance in 1879. Hence what counted was not so much the alliance system as the spirit with which it was operated. Germany's 'blank cheque' to Austria was not dictated by any alliance. After all, Germany had not always provided support when Austria asked for it. Second, the alliances were not actually operated in 1914. A member of the Triple Alliance, Italy, decided to remain neutral (and then joined the *Entente* Powers in 1915). Germany was supposed to aid Austria if Austria were attacked by Russia, but Germany declared war on Russia without this happening. As for Britain, no agreement obliged her to support France.

The alliances can be seen as both a reflection of insecurity and a contribution towards it. French fears of Germany led her to seek an alliance with Russia. The conclusion of the Franco-Russian Alliance, however, increased Germany's sense of insecurity. This was intensified by Britain's agreements with France and Russia in 1904 and 1907, creating what the Germans called 'encirclement' but which Britain and her partners regarded as 'containment' of an unpredictable Germany. Perhaps the alliances were more important for the escalation of tension that preceded the war than for the actual outbreak of war in 1914. In the July Crisis Powers consulted their interests, not their alliances.

The alliance system represented an aspect of what was often called 'international anarchy' which, it was said, turned Europe into a powder magazine needing only a spark to ignite it. The existence of sovereign states pursuing their own national interests in a highly competitive situation was bound, it was argued, to lead to war sooner or later. Yet it is clear that the explanatory power of such observations is rather limited. Why, for example, did the war come later rather than sooner? Critics of the concept also point out that this so-called 'international anarchy' had been a fact of life in European affairs since at least 1870, during which time Europe had enjoyed over 40 years of peace

Some historians see the outbreak of war as stemming from the collapse of the 'Concert of Europe', whereby the Great Powers would discuss their problems together and settle them by agreement. Certainly in 1914 some Powers were no longer willing to exercise restraint in the interests of 'Europe' as a whole. Yet the Concert had operated successfully in dealing with crises in the Near East in the 1870s and 1880s and had played a crucial role in preventing war amongst the Powers during the Balkan Wars. Why then did it fail to operate a short while later in July 1914? There was certainly no shortage of mediation proposals in 1914. Perhaps the answer is that Germany did not want a diplomatic solution, perhaps because she positively wanted war, perhaps to protect her ally.

How important was the arms race that preceded the war? It was certainly a sign of international tension, but it was also a cause of further tensions. The Anglo-German naval race had poisoned relations between those two countries. After 1912 the emphasis switched to armies. Germany, Austria-Hungary and France all increased the size of their peacetime armies between 1912 and 1914, so creating an arms race atmosphere, though the main increase in strength took place in Russia. Her defeat in the Russo-Japanese war underlined the need for reform and expansion, a process that greatly alarmed Germany.

It is hard to accept the proposition that the arms race led inevitably to war. The escalation of armaments may have made war more likely by breeding fear and suspicion – though even this is not certain, since great arms sometimes act as a deterrent. But it certainly did not make a particular war at a particular time certain.

Most historians accept that the arms race increased international tension and heightened chauvinistic feelings amongst the public in general before 1914. It is also agreed that in some states the General Staff exercised so much pressure for mobilisation that diplomats found they had little freedom of manoeuvre as the crisis deepened in late July. The fact remains, however, that some governments were more willing than others to start a war in 1914 and the reasons were political, not military.

7 Capitalism, Imperialism and Nationalism

> **KEY ISSUE** To what extent did these 'impersonal forces' lead to war?

The role of impersonal forces in the origins of the war has long been controversial. It is clear that such forces cannot explain why a specific war broke out, but they may constitute important underlying causes for war.

Some historians accept Marx's view that 'Wars are inherent in the nature of capitalism; they will only cease when the capitalist economy is abolished'. Capitalism was said to make war inevitable on two grounds. First, industrialists, especially armaments manufacturers, had a vested interest in provoking war to increase their profits or to ruin their competitors. Second, capitalist economic pressure was the driving force behind the imperialist rivalries, which in turn led to war in 1914.

Arguments such as these have the merit of simplicity but they do not take into account some of the complexities of the world of international trade and finance. It is all too easy to make generalisations about the 'wicked capitalists' who were 'warmongers' and to ignore the fact that armaments manufacturers had markets overseas which might be lost in wartime. Certainly the best interests of international bankers were served by political stability not by warfare. In July 1914, there were fears in London of a complete financial collapse if Britain became involved in war.

Anglo-German trade rivalry has been cited as an example of capitalist competition leading to war. There were certainly complaints of unfair competition and loss of markets but these were mostly in the 1890s or stemmed from trades which were particularly badly hit by German competition. In general, Britain's commercial links with Germany were growing closer from 1904 to 1914, with both sides establishing valuable markets in the other country and creating greater interdependence in manufacturing processes. Economic considerations were not the main determinant of Anglo-German relations; nor were they at the forefront of decision-making in July 1914.

A connection between imperialism and war may seem more plausible than the link with capitalism. Lenin, in particular, made a direct causal link between imperialism and war, arguing in 1916 that the war being fought amongst the Great Powers was an 'imperialist war', to effect a re-division of colonial territories. Since Germany had a prime interest in acquiring the colonies of other states, this could explain her decision for war in 1914.

Admittedly imperial rivalries had caused friction between the European Powers, as we saw with Franco-German clashes over Morocco in 1905 and 1911. But these issues had not led to war, and the problems seemed to be largely over before 1914. On the other hand, the psychological consequences of imperial rivalry, especially in terms of deepening mutual suspicion and hostility, contributed to the 'mood' of 1914. Imperialism had undoubtedly aroused nationalistic feelings.

Nationalism itself had become a more aggressive force in many of the major states by the turn of the century. This trend was fostered by the popular press and by right-wing pressure groups inspired by Social Darwinism, such as the Pan-German League, which aimed to include all Germans within Germany. The theme 'expand or decline' provided Pan-Germans with an expansionist programme at the expense of other states that was seemingly justified by the laws of nature. Also significant was Pan-Slavism, which provided justification for Russian expansion in the Balkans. Nor were only the Great Powers affected. Pan-Serbism was only one form of Balkan nationalism. Many historians have judged that a primary cause of the war in 1914 was the fact so many nationalisms were unsatisfied, so that political frontiers did not correspond to national groupings.

8 Conclusion

> **KEY ISSUE** What combination of causes best explains the outbreak of war in 1914?

The immediate causes of war are to be found in the July Crisis. This was when the crucial decisions were taken. These decisions were themselves influenced by the rise in international tension from about 1905, which was generated partly by German *Weltpolitik*, partly by the revival of Balkan crises. Further complexity inevitably arises from an examination of the broader political and economic context in which Great Power diplomacy operated. This involves consideration of the more 'impersonal forces': alliances, international anarchy, nationalism, imperialism and capitalism.

The complexity of the debate on war origins indicates that a single-cause explanation is unconvincing. It is possible, however, to identify a number of key factors. There are, perhaps, four that can be regarded as central to an explanation of the 1914 war. They are: the legacy of *Weltpolitik*; the growth of Russian power; the disruptive effect of nationalism in the Balkans; and German policy during the July Crisis. Together, these go a long way towards explaining why the First World War came about.

i) The legacy of Weltpolitik

German 'world policy' had failed by 1914 and had harmed Germany's relations with other Powers. Its failure led to a sense of frustration amongst the country's leaders and public opinion at their meagre achievements, especially when contrasted with their high expectations. Germany's overseas empire, for example, was not much bigger in 1914 than it had been in 1896. Hence Germans felt that they had not attained that position in world affairs that their economic strength seemed to warrant. They also felt insecure and indeed 'encircled' by hostile Powers, after the formation of the Triple Entente in 1907. Yet it was German foreign policy after 1905 – for example, the naval race, the crises over Morocco and Bosnia and German expansion into the Near East – that had produced this situation. It is hard to avoid the conclusion that Germany's insecurity was largely of her own making.

ii) The growth of Russian power

In the decade before 1914 Germans were alarmed not only by Russian population growth but by her army reforms and railway development. By 1916–17, the Germans believed, the Russian army would be a very formidable opponent. As A.J.P. Taylor has pointed out: 'Where most of Europe felt overshadowed by Germany, she saw the more distant Russian shadow.' Hence war in August 1914 may have been Germany's 'last chance'.

iii) Balkan Nationalism

Sarajevo was perceived as the 'last straw' as far as Austria-Hungary was concerned. The disruptive force of nationalism in south east Europe now had to be dealt with. Conflicts between the nationalities within Austria-Hungary threatened the state with dislocation, and the appeal of a Great Serbia to Serbs and Croats inside the state threatened total disintegration. Serbia's assertive nationalism was a challenge that Austria-Hungary could not ignore if she was to survive as a Great Power.

iv) German Policy in July 1914

Finally, it can be argued that German policy after the murder at Sarajevo was the last ingredient needed to produce war. Either the Germans deliberately started war, as Fischer argued, or Germany took a 'calculated risk' in encouraging the Austrians to retaliate against Serbia. This risk was not guaranteed to produce war. After all, immediate action against Serbia in retaliation for the death of the heir to the Habsburg throne might not have produced Russian retaliation. German leaders should be blamed, however, for their failure to devise 'contingency plans', or diplomatic alternatives, in case

Russia was prepared to fight. By sticking to the Schlieffen plan, a war with Russia inevitably meant a war with France (and probably with Britain) too. In view of the impact of *Weltpolitik* on international relations and of Germany's role in the July Crisis, it seems fairly clear that Germany's responsibility for causing the war was greater than that of any other Power.

v) Minor factors

A number of other factors can be considered to have played a subsidiary role in the origins of the war. Four such factors might be: the decline of the 'Concert'; the armaments race; the legacy of imperial rivalries; and the influence of domestic tensions on foreign policy decisions.

It is clear that in 1914 the destructive capacity of modern European states greatly exceeded their ability to adopt a constructive approach towards solving a serious crisis. Hence some mechanism was needed to moderate the pursuit of national self-interest. But the Great Powers failed to act in concert. Secondly, the arms race not only increased expectations of war but also led Germany to believe that she had a better chance of winning a land war in 1914 than in a few years' time. Thirdly, the imperialist rivalries of previous decades had increased animosities, affecting the attitudes not just of governments but also of public opinion and the press, contributing to the warlike mood of July 1914. Finally, the existence of domestic tensions in countries such as Germany, Austria-Hungary and Russia in the years prior to 1914 encouraged some sections of opinion, including elements in the ruling circles, to contemplate war as a relief from such tensions and a possible means of avoiding social upheaval. For a time this strategy seemed to work, as patriotism united nations as never before. It proved a delusion all the same, for the Great War led to the collapse of Germany, Austria-Hungary and Russia.

Working on Chapter 6

Your notes from this chapter should provide you with a clear summary of the main interpretations put forward to explain the First World War. Try to decide which explanations may be combined together and which are incompatible. In the final section we outlined a broad explanation which you may find acceptable – but do not feel that you have to agree with it. Try to come to at least a preliminary decision about what *you* think, and be sure you have good reasons for your view. Do you think that the events are just too complex to support any simple explanation? If so, this idea could form the basis for a very effective critique of some of the major interpretations.

Summary Diagram
The Origins of the First World War

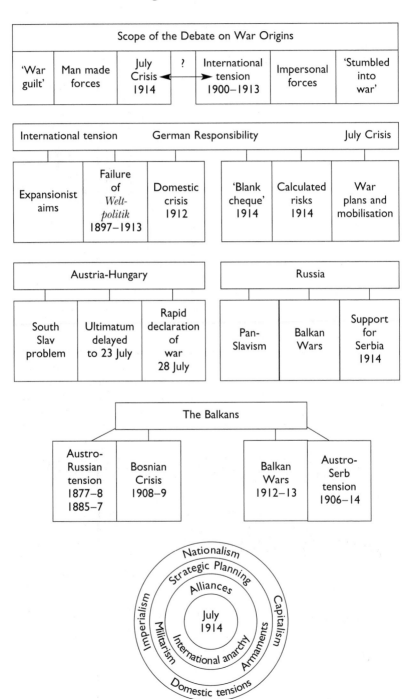

Scope of the Debate on War Origins						
'War guilt'	Man made forces	July Crisis 1914	?	International tension 1900–1913	Impersonal forces	'Stumbled into war'

International tension	German Responsibility			July Crisis

Expansionist aims	Failure of *Welt-politik* 1897–1913	Domestic crisis 1912	'Blank cheque' 1914	Calculated risks 1914	War plans and mobilisation

Austria-Hungary			Russia		
South Slav problem	Ultimatum delayed to 23 July	Rapid declaration of war 28 July	Pan-Slavism	Balkan Wars	Support for Serbia 1914

The Balkans			
Austro-Russian tension 1877–8 1885–7	Bosnian Crisis 1908–9	Balkan Wars 1912–13	Austro-Serb tension 1906–14

Answering essay questions on Chapter 6

Although the range of questions asked on this topic is fairly wide, most of them focus on one of three issues: the alliance system; the Balkans; and responsibility for causing the war.

Study the following questions:

1. To what extent was the alliance system responsible for the outbreak of the First World War?
2. 'A Balkan war that got out of control'. Is this an adequate assessment of the events of 1914?
3. How far were Russian ambitions in the Balkans the main cause of the First World War?
4. Should any one nation be seen as responsible for the outbreak of the First World War?
5. How far was German policy responsible for the outbreak of war in 1914?
6. Why did the Sarajevo murder but not the Agadir Crisis of 1911 lead to the outbreak of war?

It is worth thinking about these questions and drawing up a plan for each of them. Question 6 is the odd one out, since it focuses on 1911 as well as 1914. But notice in general how the questions require broadly the same factual knowledge. (If you are asked to assess German responsibility, you are bound to bring in Russian involvement as well, and *vice versa*. If you are asked about the alliance system, you will need to assess its importance in relation to that of other factors. If you are asked about the Balkans, you will nevertheless show that the situation there is not sufficient on its own to explain the outbreak of war between the Great Powers.) But the emphasis you give to certain factors must be determined in relation to the actual question asked.

By all means make up your mind on the basic issues, but do not prepare a 'stock' examination answer on this topic, to be used regardless of the particular question asked. Instead, you have to think logically, defining the terms of the question and breaking the overall question down into smaller, more manageable ones, on each of which you should have a paragraph.

In addition, you must attempt to see things in perspective. A good answer on the July Crisis will almost certainly make references to months and years before July 1914. Many students wear 'blinkers' and fail to see connections between specific topics, but the best students see individual issues within the broad sweep of a wider period of history. Hence it is worth studying the following questions which cover the whole period of this book:

7. What effects did colonial rivalries have on relations between the Great Powers in the period from 1871 to 1914?
8. What benefits did France and Russia look for when making their alliance of 1894, and how far were their expectations realised during the next 20 years?

9. Is the term 'international anarchy' a satisfactory description of international relations between 1871 and 1914?
10. Why did it prove impossible to solve the problems created by Balkan nationalism before 1914?
11. How and why had Europe become an armed camp by 1914?
12. Explain the fact that in 1914 the international alliances, which had previously served the cause of peace, now helped to produce war.

None of these questions is easy, but it is worth grappling with them. If you do so, you will a) be prepared for broad essay questions, b) have developed your understanding of the sweep of international relations, and c) be able to see the specific issues in their true context.

Further Reading

There are literally hundreds of books on international relations and imperialism in the period 1870–1914. You will therefore be spoilt for choice!

'Access' books which are complementary to this one, and look at aspects of the issues included here, are **Andrina Stiles and Alan Farmer**, *The Unification of Germany* (Hodder & Stoughton, 2nd edition, 2001); and **Frank McDonough**, *The British Empire 1815–1914* (Hodder & Stoughton, 1994); and **Robert Pearce**, *Britain and the European Powers, 1865–1914* (Hodder & Stoughton, 1996).

If you wish to consult wide-ranging textbooks on the period, the following are recommended: **Norman Stone**, *Europe Transformed, 1878–1919* (Blackwell, 2nd edition, 2000) and **Martin Pugh** (ed), *A Companion to Modern European History, 1871–1945* (Blackwell, 1997)

Wide-ranging studies of international diplomacy include **F. R. Bridge and R. Bullen**, *The Great Powers and the European States System, 1815–1914*, (Longman, 1980) and **John Lowe**, *The Great Powers, Imperialism and the German Problem, 1865–1925* (Routledge, 1994). **Paul Kennedy**, *The Realities Behind Diplomacy* (Fontana, 1981), is written with wonderful clarity and is especially valuable for its coverage of 'unspoken assumptions'. Books specifically on imperialism include **M.E. Chamberlain**, *The Scramble for Africa* (Longman, 1974), which includes some useful source material, and **Andrew Porter**, *European Imperialism, 1860–1914* (Macmillan, 1994).

On Bismarck's diplomacy, **J.A.S. Grenville**, *Europe Reshaped, 1848–1878* (Blackwell, 2nd edition, 2000), is a masterly study. See also the biography by **Edgar Feuchtwanger**, *Bismarck* (Routledge, 2002).

On the causes of 1914–18 war, there are numerous good books to consult. One of the best is **James Joll**, *The Origins of the First World War* (Longman, 1984). Shorter and more succinct is **David Stevenson**, *The Outbreak of the First World War: 1914 in Perspective* (Macmillan, 1997). There are also several collections of essays which are well worth dipping into: these include **Keith Wilson** (ed), *Decisions for War, 1914* (UCL Press, 1995), **R.J.W. Evans and H. Pogge. von Strandmann** (eds), *The Coming of the First World War* (OUP, 1988), and **H.W. Koch** (ed), *The Origins of the First World War* (Macmillan 2nd edition, 1984). **Gordon Martel**, *The Origins of the First World War*, in the Seminar Studies series (Longman, 3rd edition, 2002), includes a selection of source materials.

For Germany's role in producing the Great War, there are many studies of the Kaiser. One of the best is **James Retallack**, *Germany in the Age of Kaiser Wilhelm II* (Macmillan, 1996). A fine series of volumes on the roles of individual countries has been published by Macmillan. These include **V.R. Berghahn**, *Germany and the Approach of War in 1914* (1973); **J.F.V. Keiger,** *France and the Origins of the First World War* (1983); **Zara Steiner**, *Britain and the Origins of the First World War* (1977); **S.R. Williamson**, *Austria-Hungary and the Origins of the First World War* (1991); and **D.C.B. Lieven**, *Russia and the Origins of the First World War* (1983).

Index